DOSTOEVSKY'S SECRET CODE

The Allegory of Elijah the Prophet

Yuri I. Marmeladov

Translated by Jay MacPherson

Coronado Press   1987

ISBN: 0-87291-171-3

©1987 by Coronado Press

All rights reserved. No part of this publication may be reproduced or transmitted in any form or by any means, electronic or mechanical, including photocopy, recording, or any information storage and retrieval system, without permission in writing from the publisher.

Coronado Press
P.O. Box 3232
Lawrence, Kansas 66044

Printed in the United States of America

Like a whirlwind the chariot races –
The living spokes spin round and round.
Above the sea of frightened faces
A rider's trumpet sounds.

– Aleksandr Blok, *The Fire*

Translator's Preface

Professor Marmeladov did not complete *Dostoevsky's Secret Code* by the time of his death in 1984. The present English edition is based on the manuscript which he left behind. It was necessary to fill in many lacunae, especially in the notes, and parts of the manuscript are barely legible due to wine stains and smudges caused by cigar ashes. Leaves 88-93 are missing altogether. Judging by leaf 87B, these pages dealt with "A Nasty Story" and *The Humiliated and the Injured*. Those who knew Yuri Il'ich will recall how often he would mutter, "What did Bakhtin know?!" as he casually ripped a page from one of his own essays in order to roll another cigar. Professor Marmeladov's passing is a great loss to the Slavic community and to all devoted readers of Dostoevsky. The story of his emigration to America, his shock and amazement at the quality of American education, his subsequent struggle with heart problems and alcoholism, and his final demise beneath the wheels of a furniture truck on New York's Brooklyn Bridge (extolled by Mayakovsky) is familiar to all and we need not dwell on it here. Various chapters in Professor Marmeladov's study of Dostoevsky were rejected by journals including *The Slavic and East European Journal*, *Slavic Review* and *Russkaia literatura*. Although the quality of Professor Marmeladov's scholarship does not meet the high standards of these prestigious publications, we nevertheless hope and trust that the reader will glean something new from his work. He was always acutely aware of his own shortcomings and spoke of his work as "a monument to my own sloth and ignorance." He insisted that "publish or perish" is only a myth, and the present publication serves to illustrate that one can indeed "publish *and* perish."

Professor Marmeladov's extremely terse expository style demands far too much from the reader, and in an age of space exploration and high technology his penchant for church terminology is anachronistic and annoying. Professor Fridlender often pointed this out to him, and I remember well how in reply Yuri Il'ich would simply stretch out his arms and mumble (cigar in teeth): "Crucify me!" The poor writing style engendered many problems in rendering the work into English, but I feel that I have accomplished this task as well as can be expected in the given circumstances. I owe a great debt of gratitude to Patrick Gibbons, who provided invaluable assistance in compiling the notes, and to Ronald Schwartz, whose generous support made this publication possible. Others whom we wish to thank for their support and assistance include (in reverse alphabetic order): Ruth Zernova, Francis Whitfield, Steve Watkins, Anatoly Vishevsky, Eileen Thurman, Marina Steblin-Kamenskaya, Regina Snyder, Hilary Shadroui, Ilya Serman, Jakub Szczupak, Miluse Saskova-Pierce, Wlodzimierz Rybarkiewicz, Karen Ryan-Hayes, Howard Robertson, James Rice, Elwira Pniewska, Temira Pachmuss, Aldona Nowicka-Schwartz, James Ogdie, Evgenii Frankovich Nizelik, Ernst Neizvestny, Joseph Mozur, Molly Molloy, Jay Minn, Czeslaw Milosz, Wolfgang Mieder, Zofia Michalik, Olga Markov-Belaeff, Randall Magee, Nadiya Maksutovna Mingazetdinova, Hugh McLean, Lev Loseff, Katrin Loczy, Barbara Laudon, Pacho Lane, Edwin Kreuzer, Piotr Kolyszko, Anna Kolyszko, Stanislaw Kielbasa, Mary Kirk, Edward Kasinec, Simon Karlinsky, Roy Jones, William Harkins, Ljiljana Grubisic, Gail Groza, Linda Grimes, Tatiana Gorokhovskaya, Scott Filar, Garland Durham, Jeff Douglas, Paula Dietrich, Michael Dasaro, Ken Czerwinski, Brett Cooke, Joseph Conrad, Steve Cohn, Paula Chertok, Richard Carter, Boris Briker, Asta Aristov, Anthony Anemone, Germann Andreev, Sam Anderson.

Jay MacPherson
St. Petersburg, Florida

CONTENTS

Introduction: Elijah the Prophet in
    Russian Tradition.................................... 1

Part One: Elijah the Prophet in *Crime*
    and Punishment..................................... 7

Part Two: *The Village of Stepanchikovo*
    and *The Possessed*................................ 26

Part Three: "Mr. Prokharchin"........................ 52

Part Four: *The Landlady* and *The Idiot*............... 66

Part Five: *The Eternal Husband*....................... 91

Notes.. 103

Introduction: Elijah the Prophet in Russian Tradition

> *Even as thou wast carried by the fiery chariot, as in an earthquake, into the heavens and, bestowed with the fire-inspired gift of miracles, thou becamst immortal, never knowing death until thou hast prophesied the end of all creatures and things, so come to us now, Elijah the Tishbite, bestowing upon us the guidance of your admonitions.*
>
> — *Mineia prazdnichnaia*

When thunder rumbled overhead in prerevolutionary Russia, it was a common cliché to remark: "There goes Elijah the Prophet in his chariot across the clouds." Thunder and lightning were believed to be the special provenance of Elijah, and uneducated peasants expected a thunderstorm each year on Elijah's feast day (July 20, Old Style).[1] The young nihilist Bazarov in *Fathers and Sons* speaks scornfully of this folk belief as a reflection of Russia's backwardness:

> "... The people imagine that when it thunders the prophet Elijah's riding across the sky in his chariot. What then? Are we to agree with them?..." [2]

Goncharov's *Oblomov* provides further testimony to a widespread familiarity with the folklore of Elijah:

> The thunderstorms there are nothing to fear; they are only beneficial. They always come at the same established time, almost never forgetting Elijah's Day, as though to confirm the well-known belief of the folk.[3]

The belief is truly ancient, rooted in pre-Christian, pagan lore surrounding the foremost god in Slavic myth, the thunder god Perun. After Russia's conversion in 988, the important functions of Perun were in part transferred to Elijah, giving him a special significance in the nation's new Christian pantheon. Elijah was even made the central hero of epic songs about the conversion, although his true identity and the religious underpinnings of the songs later became obscured as they were passed from generation to generation for hundreds of years. By about the sixteenth century, he was thoroughly russified, depicted in the epic songs as a mighty warrior from the town of Murom.[4]

Dostoevsky clearly perceived the importance of Elijah as a specifically Russian folk and religious symbol. Obsessed with the problem of Russia's national identity, with "the Russian soul," he repeatedly weaves the *Russian* image of Elijah the Prophet deep into the fabric of his highly symbolic fiction. In fact, it is no exaggeration to say that Elijah is the foundation upon which a number of Dostoevsky's works are constructed. Before turning to Dostoevsky's fiction, however, it is necessary to briefly survey the lore pertaining to Elijah in Russian church and folkloric tradition.

No mythic songs or tales about Elijah's Slavic predecessor Perun are now extant. Possibly they were never written down. The tradition of written literature was brought to Russia by the Church, and the activity of preserving texts in written form tended to be seen as a sacred function of the Church or the State. Even if any mythic texts were recorded, they were likely to fall victim to time and the elements or to the heavy hand of the Church, which monopolised the copying tradition for centuries and campaigned persistently against intrusions of paganism in Christian belief. Thus, information about Perun must be gleaned from brief allusions to the "vile pagan gods" in early chronicles and sermons and from *The Song of Prince Igor*, the only surviving fragment of the secular epic from the early Kievan period.[5]

Perun's name lives on in contemporary Slavic languages as a term for a lightning bolt (Russian *perun*, Polish *piorun* etc.). The oak was his sacred tree, as attested by a reference to "Perun's Oak" (*Perunov dub*) in an early chronicle.[6] The aurochs (*tur*), a kind of bison that is now extinct, was venerated in association with the thunder god. As the thunderbearer, Perun was seen as a warrior god who carried a sword or cudgel; but as provider of rain, he was also viewed as a source of life and fertility. According to a chronicle account of the conversion of Novgorod, when the pagan idol of Perun was thrown into the Volkhov River, a demon inside the idol threw the god's cudgel up onto a bridge as it drifted downstream. The pious chronicler notes that senseless people continue to use the cudgel to beat one another, "bringing great joy to the demons."[7] The twelfth-century *Song of Prince Igor* portrays one Russian prince as a fierce aurochs who rains arrows on the enemy and "thunders" with his swords, while his helmet "flashes" like lightning. The heads of the enemy can be seen lying wherever he bounds:

> Fierce aurochs Vsevolod!
> You stand your ground,
> You spray arrows on the foe,
> You thunder against helmets
> With your swords of burnished steel!
> Wherever the aurochs leaps,
> Flashing with his golden helmet,
> There lie pagan Polovtsian heads:
> Their Avar helmets lie,
> Cleft by your tempered sabres,
> Fierce aurochs Vsevolod![8]

This metaphoric portrayal, doubtless a cliché of the Kievan epic tradition, derives ultimately from ritual songs in which Perun was depicted as a running aurochs who brings fertility wherever he bounds. These pagan songs are also the antecedents for Russian New Year's and springtime songs about Elijah, Yarilo and a goat (a horned animal symbolizing fertility, like the aurochs), who bring an abundant harvest wherever they step.[9]

The pagan Slavic pantheon also included a dragon, who was probably portrayed in myth as the perennial rival of Perun.[10] His name has survived until recent times in a Bulgarian song about St. George and the dragon and in a Serbian fairytale about a certain "Troyan" who visits a woman each night, leaving when the roosters crow, just before sunrise. But when the woman's husband (or brother in one variant) slits the roosters' tongues, he stays too long and is melted by the sun.[11] In one variant Troyan has three heads; in another his role is played by a dragon.[12] In his different guises, the monster in this tale is a variation on the "fiery dragon" (*ognennyi zmei*) who, according to Slavic folk belief, visits women, especially widows, at night.[13] Another vestige of the pagan Slavic dragon is the name of ancient earthen embankments along the Dnepr River in the present-day Ukraine: "Troyan's Embankments" (*Troianovy valy*), also known as "The Dragon's Embankments" (*Zmievy valy*).[14]

With a dragon and thunder god in their own mythic tradition, the Slavs' attention was naturally drawn to Elijah the Prophet and the dragon of the Apocalypse. In 1st Kings 17-21, Elijah is given the divine power to control the rainfall, and he invokes fire from heaven to ignite a burnt offering in a duel with the priests of Baal. He brings down the same lightning fire onto the soldiers of Ahaziah in 2nd Kings 1. In 2nd Kings 2, Elijah ascends to Heaven on a fiery chariot drawn by fiery steeds. The chariot rises in a whirlwind, and Slavic church texts also speak of an earthquake which accompanied the Prophet's miraculous ascent:

> Elijah, blessed of God, thou hast seen in the

earthquake and the whirlwind God's coming, which enlightened thee of old. For, riding on the four-steed chariot, thou hast crossed vast expanses, filled with wonderment and inspired by God.[15]

In Revelation 11, two "witnesses" oppose a "beast from the netherworld," one of the apocalyptic symbols of evil who is sometimes equated with the dragon in Chapter 12. According to Orthodox Church tradition, the two witnesses are Elijah and Enoch the Righteous. A number of religious texts, such as *The Revelation of Methodius of Patara*, refer specifically to Elijah and Enoch. According to Methodius, whose *Revelation* was well known in Kievan Russia, Elijah and Enoch will expose the Antichrist before the Last Judgment.[16] In St. John's account, the two witnesses are said to have the power to control the rain while they deliver their prophecies.

Elijah's associations with fire, rain, lightning and a god-like trek across the sky made it inevitable that the Slavs would perceive him as a Christian counterpart to their pagan god of thunder and lightning. This perception was reinforced by the fact that Elijah's feast day (July 20, Old Style) comes at a time of summer when thunderstorms are frequent. The Elijah-Perun connection seems to be reflected in the procedure that was followed, according to a chronicle account, when the Kiev Prince Oleg concluded a treaty with Constantinople in 945. The pagan members of the prince's retinue swore to the treaty by the idol of Perun, while those who were Christians took an oath in the Church of Elijah the Prophet.[17]

Prince Vladimir's conversion of the Kievan state in 988 gave rise to an epic song in which Elijah comes to Kiev and delivers Vladimir's city from a huge, living pagan idol – probably the idol of his predecessor Perun. The idol was patterned in part after the living idol of Revelation 13, and the song depicted the Christianization of Russia as a final, apocalyptic "seventh millenium" of the pagan gods. Another episode of the oral epic – possibly in the same song – portrayed the demise of the dragon Troyan, who was associated with the seven-headed dragon of Revelation 12. This episode is reflected in *The Song of Prince Igor*, which alludes to "the seventh millenium of Troyan" in an account that is fashioned after the earlier song about the conversion.[18]

When the prophet-hero eventually came to be perceived as the Russian warrior Elijah of Murom, vestiges of his Biblical identity nevertheless remained. For example, at the end of one Belorussian prose version of the tale, Elijah rises into the skies in order to take charge of the thunder and lightning.[19] In the early history of the tale, Elijah received a staff from St. John, who, according to numerous church texts, is to oppose the Antichrist alongside Elijah and Enoch.[20] Like Elijah, St. John later underwent russification, and versions of the song recorded in recent centuries portray him as a giant pilgrim (*Ivanishche*) with a staff that weighs over a ton. The spiritual power and authority of the Apostle was reinterpreted as sheer brute strength.[21]

Dostoevsky, nevertheless, perceived the essentially religious basis for the song about Elijah and St. John. In the drafts for *A Raw Youth*, the pilgrim Makar Ivanov (a sort of literary Ivanishche) prophesies the advent of Elijah, Enoch and the Antichrist.[22] Dostoevsky's notebooks refer to Ivanishche and Elijah of Murom (the russified Prophet, hero of the epic song in its recent form).[23] He sees Elijah of Murom as the folkloric apotheosis of the Russian spirit, and in works such as *The Village of Stepanchikovo* and *The Landlady* he weaves reminiscences of this epic hero into an intricate network of symbols associated with Elijah the Prophet. It is to this Elijah symbolism, a central allegory throughout Dostoevsky's fiction, that we should now turn.

Part One: Elijah the Prophet in *Crime and Punishment*

> *"But the thunder has struck. I accept the ordeal of condemnation and public disgrace. I want to suffer and through suffering I will be cleansed!"*
> *"A new man has been resurrected in me! He was concealed inside me and would have never appeared if it hadn't been for this thunder."*
> – Dmitrii Karamazov

Crime and Punishment is the story of a murderer's path to confession. An inner, spiritual awareness of the necessity to accept suffering for his sins leads Raskol'nikov to confess his crime, even though he knows there is no legally incriminating evidence against him. In Dostoevsky's view, all men share the spirit of Christ, and the story of Rodion Raskol'nikov is an allegory about the spiritual path of mankind as a whole. His crime can be compared with original sin and the fall of man in the Bible.[1] A clerk at the police station remarks that the murderer escaped capture because the building where the old pawnbroker lived is "a Noah's ark" [83].[2] The clerk simply means that the building is large, with plenty of places where the murderer might hide. But there is also a suggestion of the ark that saved the human race after Adam's fall and the corruption of his descendants – a vague hint at the promise of salvation which looms before Raskol'nikov throughout the novel.

Other Biblical symbols mark Raskol'nikov's path and show that he is following in Christ's footsteps toward suffering and redemption. He visits Sonia at the Kapernaumovs', whose name is derived from Capernaum, one of a series of towns Christ visited before his crucifixion, healing the afflicted and raising Lazarus from the dead. In the novel, Kapernaumov and his wife are both lame and they have a speech impediment; Kapernaumova is half deaf, their eldest child stutters, and their other children are sickly; the derelict building in which they live, the dwelling of cripples and a prostitute, recalls the Biblical Capernaum, the fate of which Christ compared to Sodom (Matthew 11:23-24). Of course, it is at the Kapernaumovs' that Sonia reads to Raskol'nikov about the resurrection of Lazarus.

Following Christ, Raskol'nikov "takes on the cross" given him by Sonia when he goes to confess. He then bows at the crossroads (*perekrestok*: from *krest* 'cross') and kisses the ground.[3] A bystander speculates that he is a pilgrim about to set out for Jerusalem, the city of Christ's crucifixion. On the way to the police station, Raskol'nikov thinks about "drinking the cup." He may have in mind only the "cup" of his own sufferings, but the parallel with the "bitter cup" of Christ is unmistakable. Like Mary Magdalene, the prostitute who followed Christ to his crucifixion, Sonia follows Raskol'nikov to the police station and later to Siberia. An early draft states that she follows him "to Golgotha."[4] When he is sick and in delirium in Siberia, Sonia waits by his side, much as Mary Magdalene waited at Christ's tomb.[5] Finally, his spiritual resurrection occurs shortly after Easter, the holiday of Christ's resurrection.

As he struggles with the nihilistic idea that has taken possession of his mind, leading him to kill the old pawnbroker, Raskol'nikov encounters other "great sinners" in whom he might see a reflection of his own fallen spirit. They include the lecher Svidrigailov, whose tormented conscience finally leads him to suicide, and the drunk Marmeladov, who pleads to be "crucified" and follows a seemingly suicidal path with his alcoholic's "cup of sorrow" in hand. Alongside these fallen spirits the murderer encounters representatives of communal authority with whom he duels and to whom he is irresistibly drawn throughout the novel. Prominent among them are Porfirii Petrovich, the wily police examiner who torments the murderer with insinuations and subtle mockery, and Il'ia Petrovich "Pórokh," the assistant police superintendent to whom Raskol'nikov eventually confesses. Through a series of word-plays, allusions and imagery associated with Elijah the Prophet, Pórokh is made a symbol of divine retribution and the law of God.

Il'ia Petrovich figures in three highly symbolic episodes: first, when Raskol'nikov is summoned to the police station for not repaying his debt to his landlady; second, when he dreams that Il'ia Petrovich is beating his landlady; and third, when he finally confesses during his second visit to the police station. *Pórokh* ('Gunpowder') is a nickname given to Il'ia Petrovich by his comrades in the army because of his fiery temperament. The police superintendent first mentions the nickname in a passage that juxtaposes the words *porók* ('vice,' 'crime') and *pórokh* ('gunpowder'):

"Poverty is no vice, my friend! But, as we all know, you're gunpowder. No tolerance for these little slights..." [80]

The similarity between *porók* and *pórokh* points to the underlying word-play between *Il'ia Pórokh* and *Il'ia Prorók* ('Elijah the Prophet'), the lord of thunder and lightning in Russian folk belief.[6]

The nickname *Porokh*, resembling *prorok* ('prophet') and eliciting associations with fire, is appropriate for a symbolic Elijah the Prophet. But for Dostoevsky and his Petersburg readers the nickname also elicited associations with the Church of Elijah the Prophet at the Powderworks (*Tserkov' Ilii-proroka na Porokhovykh*) and with the local custom of making an annual pilgrimage to the powderworks on the feast day of Elijah.[7] Goncharov repeatedly alludes to this custom in *Oblomov*, where Elijah the

Prophet looms as a central symbol of Judgment:

> They talked about Elijah's Friday and about the annual outings made on foot to the Powderworks, about the holiday at the Smolensk Cemetery in Kolpino. [*Oblomov*, Part 4, Chapter 1]
>
> "[...] Just the other day, on Elijah's Friday, we went to the Powderworks."
> "Well, do a lot of people gather there?" asked Oblomov [...]
> "No, this year there weren't many. In the morning it rained, although later it cleared up. In good weather there's a lot of people."
> [*Oblomov*, Part 3, Chapter 2] [8]

Dostoevsky endows his Il'ia Porokh with the fiery attributes of the thunder-wielding prophet. He has a "lightning gaze" (a "thunderous gaze" in one of the notebooks).[9] He spews a rain of saliva when he grows excited, and he "lets loose with all his thunderbolts" against a brothel keeper who is summoned to the police station.[10] When the superintendent arrives and finds Porokh in a rage, he exclaims: "Again that rumbling, thunder, and lightning; that whirlwind and hurricane once again!"[11] The whirlwind and hurricane recall the fiery whirlwind in which the Biblical Elijah ascends to heaven.

Porokh's other fiery traits include a red beard and a cigarette which elicits a complaint from Raskol'nikov. Porokh "flames," "boils" and "burns" when he is angry. He speaks in a thundering voice and his "lightning" is mentioned again and again: "It was as though thunder and lightning had struck in the office...;" "she [the brothel keeper] was all atremble beneath Porokh's thunder and lightning" [78]. His rank, assistant superintendent, is a playful parallel to that of Elijah the Prophet, who as a figure of divine retribution might be called an assistant of

God. In the context of Dostoevsky's symbolism, the term for 'superintendent' (*nadziratel'*: literally, 'overseer') is suggestive of an all-seeing god. As Georgii Meier has noted, the superintendent's name, Nikodim Fomich, has a decidedly Biblical coloring.[12] When Porokh instructs Raskol'nikov, "Please be quiet! You are in a government office!" (*"Izvol'te ma-a-lchat'! Vy v prisutstvii!"*) [77], a second, symbolic meaning is implied by the author: "You are in His presence." (*Prisutstvie* can mean both 'office' and 'presence'.)

Raskol'nikov's route toward confession – the spiral staircase leading up to the police station – is a spiritual ascent into the realm of divine wrath and mercy. The spiral shape of the stairway evokes once again the whirlwind which carried Elijah into heaven. Raskol'nikov's head "spins" as he climbs the stairs, reinforcing the associations with Elijah's whirlwind. A symbolic spiritual significance for the episode at the police station is intimated by the repetition of words derived from *dukh*, which means both 'odor' and 'spirit'. Raskol'nikov "catches his breath" (*perevel dukh*) when he reaches the station, located on the fifth and highest story. The air is stifling (*dukhota*). The room smells heavily of the brothel keeper Luiza Ivanovna's perfume (*dukhí*).

The spiral staircase also figures in one of Raskol'nikov's dreams, where its spiritual significance is quite clear. Neither asleep nor awake, he sees a series of images *whirling* before him: a tavern, a billiard table, a tobacco shop, a staircase strewn with egg shells, and the belfry of the Church of the Ascension. He hears "the sound of Sunday bells" (or, literally, "Resurrection" bells: *voskresnyi zvon kolokolov*) [210]. The vision incorporates images of a corrupt netherworld and a higher spiritual realm, with the stairway as a bridge between the two planes. The stairway is the one which leads to the police station, as suggested by the egg shells which litter the stairs when Raskol'nikov ascends to the police station to confess to Porokh in Part Six. His dream signifies a tortuous ascent from sin to redemption.

The first episode at the police station is an allegorical portrayal of Raskol'nikov's spiritual torment. It is his first opportunity to confess, but he remains barricaded in his fortress of pride and weathers the storm of abuse which the symbolic Elijah the Prophet rains down on him. As Georgii Meier has shown, the heavily perfumed Luiza Ivanovna is a symbol of Raskol'nikov's sinful, fallen spirit.[13] Her dress, which is like a balloon and occupies almost half the room, gives her an airy, buoyant, amorphous aspect. The narrator refers to her with the formula *pyshnaia dama*, which means 'flamboyantly dressed lady' in the given context, but is suggestive of fluffiness and airiness. Luiza Ivanovna takes buoyant little leaps as she walks, and she "flies" out of the room. She is half German and her speech is a comical hodgepodge of German and Russian, while Raskol'nikov is evidently steeped in German letters and is called a "German hatter" by a drunk who makes fun of his hat near the beginning of the novel [7].[14] In her heavy German accent Luiza Ivanovna spills words "like peas," a comparison which is intended once more to establish a symbolic link with Raskol'nikov, who "smashed" (*ogoróshil*, derived from *gorókh* 'peas') the pawnbroker's head and whose altruistic, utopian scheme to get rich is alluded to symbolically as "thoughts about Tsar Gorokh" ('Tsar Peas,' emperor of a proverbial Neverneverland).[15]

The scandal that was caused in Luiza Ivanovna's "noble house" by her "ignoble guest" parodies Raskol'nikov's crime, which is the result of nihilistic ideas infecting his spirit. The intruder who ran riot at Luiza Ivanovna's is a hack writer. Symbolically, he is linked with the intellectual, reasoning side of Raskol'nikov's nature and with the ideas that have gained possession of Raskol'nikov's spirit. The connection between the hack writer and the "former student" Raskol'nikov is brought out in the same scene by Il'ia Petrovich:

> "That's the way they are, these hack writers, literati, students and prophets... Tfoo!" [79]
>
> "Here you are, sir! Just take a look: Mr. Writer here, or Student, that is – former student – won't pay the money he owes, he's written all sorts of I.O.U.'s, he won't vacate his apartment, constant complaints are coming in against him, and he deigns to take offense because I've lit up my cigarette in his presence!" [80]

Luiza Ivanovna's "noble house" is evidently a brothel, but she stands before Elijah Porokh persistently asserting her innocence. She symbolizes Raskol'nikov's spirit as he stands before the eternal tribunal of the Lord, refusing to confess his guilt.

Luiza Ivanovna's remarks concerning the "nobility" of her house and the "ignobility" of her guest refer symbolically to Raskol'nikov himself.[16] When he returns to the police station near the end of the novel, Il'ia Petrovich makes repeated allusions to his noble background [407-8]. These words doubtless ring ironically in the ears of the murderer. When Raskol'nikov bows down at the crossroads on his way to confess, bystanders remark:

> "One of the nobility!" somebody noted with authority.
> "Nowadays it's hard to tell who's a noble and who isn't." [405]

The police summon Raskol'nikov to the station because of his debt to his landlady, Zarnitsyna. However, as Meier notes, the Russian word *khoziaika* means not only 'landlady,' but also 'mistress' (i.e. 'mistress of a

13

household') and so suggests that Raskol'nikov has neglected not only a financial debt, but also his duty to his inner "mistress," or conscience.[17] At the beginning of the novel, the narrator paraphrases Raskol'nikov's thoughts, stating that he was not afraid of *any* landlady [5]. But why should he fear any other landlady besides the one to whom he owes money? This rather strange display of bravado hints at the landlady's second function as a symbol of Raskol'nikov's conscience, or spiritual "mistress." In addition, she is an *assessorsha* – literally, an assessor's widow; but on the symbolic plane she is Raskol'nikov's "moral assessor." Her widowed state points to a link with the realm beyond death, a concern for the eternal and divine.

The landlady's name in the early drafts is Sof'ia, the highly symbolic name later attached to Marmeladov's daughter.[18] Despite the reassignment of names, the landlady remains another symbol of *Sophia*, the Divine Wisdom. Her surname, Zarnitsyna, is derived from *zarnitsa*, a term for sheet lightning or the glow which accompanies a bolt of lightning. After his first visit to the police station, Raskol'nikov dreams that Il'ia Petrovich is brutally beating Zarnitsyna on the stairway outside his room. Her terrible "howling, gnashing and weeping" are reminiscent of hellish, apocalyptic tortures. It is as though "the world had been turned upside down"; or as though the Last Judgment and the end of the world were approaching. When the groans and cries of the landlady have stopped, Raskol'nikov lies in terror for half an hour, unaware that he has only been dreaming [90-91]. Only the symbolic roles of Il'ia Petrovich and Zarnitsyna give this nightmare a clear meaning. Raskol'nikov's conscience, symbolized by the landlady, is tormented by a symbolic Elijah the Prophet. The quiet realizations of Raskol'nikov's conscience glow like sheet lightning beneath the bolts of divine vengeance.[19] When the servant woman Nastas'ia (her name is from Greek *Anastasia* 'Resurrection') comes to Raskol'nikov's room and illuminates the darkness with her candle (*svet ozaril komnatu*),[20] he asks her who was beating the landlady. She replies that no beating took place. According to her, this is only "the blood crying out" in Raskol'nikov [92]. The reader inevitably perceives the double meaning which was not intended by Nastas'ia: it is the blood spilled by Raskol'nikov which cries out; that is, his conscience.

Two weeks pass between the murder and Raskol'nikov's confession. Throughout this time, the weather in Petersburg is unbearably hot and muggy. The stifling air bears down on Raskol'nikov physically, while the weight of his crime bears down on his spirit. But on the fourteenth day the weather finally changes. That evening, in his last interview with Raskol'nikov, Porfirii Petrovich remarks with characteristic cunning, referring as much to Raskol'nikov's spiritual state as to the weather:

> "Going for a stroll now? Should be a fine evening. If only there's no storm. But then again, that would actually be better. It would freshen things up..." [352]

That night, a spectacular thunderstorm unleashes itself over Petersburg. The rain comes down "like a waterfall," lashing the ground for hours. Lightning strikes time after time, and the tremendous glow lasts up to five seconds [384]. Raskol'nikov spends the whole night outdoors in the storm, and it is at this time that he finally decides to confess:

> His suit was in a horrible state: all muddy, torn and tattered after the whole night in the rain. His face was almost unrecognizable from fatigue, the bad weather, physical exhaustion and the struggle with himself which had continued for nearly twenty-four hours. He had spent the whole night alone, God

knows where. But at least he had made up his mind. [395]

After his thorough drenching in the thunderstorm, Raskol'nikov visits his mother and his sister Dunia, who speaks of "washing away" his crime [399]. Then he confesses that evening to Il'ia Porokh, the symbolic Elijah the Prophet, master of thunder and lightning. The thunderstorm is the spiritual storm of Elijah the Prophet which purifies the heart. Dostoevsky has in mind not only the general association of Elijah and thunderstorms in popular Russian lore, but also the specific folk belief that Elijah will unleash a storm each year on his feast day, July 20. The action in *Crime and Punishment* gets underway "at the beginning of July" [5]. If we assume this means the first week of the month (July 1-7), then the day of the storm and of Raskol'nikov's confession is July 15-21 (the fifteenth day in the novel); i.e., on or near the feast day of Elijah. One can probably assume that the storm, in Dostoevsky's conception, begins on the eve of Elijah's Day and that Raskol'nikov confesses to Il'ia Porokh on July 20.[21]

Instead of this symbolic cleansing by water in the thunderstorm, Dostoevsky had earlier planned a purification by fire. The notebooks refer to a housefire in which Raskol'nikov helps to save the tenants. Afterwards, he returns home to his mother, all scorched and singed, much as he comes back dishevelled and weatherbeaten by the thunderstorm in the final version. Then, still covered with soot from the fire, he goes to confess to Il'ia Porokh, who says: "Why are you all charred? Oh yes, of course! Good Lord!"[22] The notebooks also refer to a vision of Christ and to a whirlwind (*vikhr'*) at the time of the fire.[23] Like the hurricane and whirlwind mentioned by Nikodim Fomich in describing Il'ia Porokh, this whirlwind was doubtless associated with the fiery whirlwind of Elijah the Prophet. Together with lightning storms, housefires were the special provenance of Elijah in Russian folk belief, and the housefire in the early drafts was evidently planned as a trial in which Raskol'nikov attains to a vision of Divine Truth as he experiences the whirling flames of the prophet's fire.[24]

Traces of this early housefire motif are discernible at several points in the novel, including the first episode at the police station. Exhausted by his inner spiritual struggle, Raskol'nikov has grown indifferent to everything around him: "Even if at that very moment he had been condemned to burn, he wouldn't have even flinched..." [81] A further intimation of the purifying function of the prophet's fire is Nikodim Fomich's praise of Porokh:

> "[...] a most noble man, I assure you, but he's gunpowder, gunpowder! He flares up, boils up, burns up – and that's it! It's all over! And as a result there's only the gold of the heart!" [80]

The phrase "as a result" (*v rezul'tate*) suggests that the "gold of the heart" refers to the heart of the suspect as well as that of Il'ia Petrovich. Of course, Nikodim Fomich is unaware of this *double entendre*, which was planted by the author himself. Porokh's fire purifies the hearts of his suspects like gold in a furnace, recalling the evocation of Elijah in Malachi 3:2-3:

> ...and who shall stand when he appeareth? for he is like a refiner's fire and like fullers' soap: And he shall sit as a refiner and purifier of silver, and he shall purify the sons of Levi, and purge them as gold and silver, that they may offer unto the Lord an offering in righteousness.

Yet another subtle allusion to the fiery whirlwind of Elijah can be discerned in the newspaper headlines which Raskol'nikov scans in the Crystal Palace as he looks for reports of the murder:

> Raskol'nikov sat down and began to search: "Izler – Izler – Aztecs – Aztecs – Izler – Bartola – Massimo – Aztecs – Izler... The devil! Ah, here are some newsbriefs: Woman Falls Down Stairs – Merchant Burns Up From Spirits [*meshchanin sgorel s vina*][25] – Fire in Peski – Fire on Petersburg Side – another fire on Petersburg Side – another fire on Petersburg Side – Izler – Izler – Izler – Izler – Massimo... Ah, here it is..." [124]

Bartola and Massimo were dwarves who were exhibited in Petersburg in 1865, touted as the last living Aztecs.[26] They were doubtless imposters. Ivan Ivanovich Izler operated an amusement park outside Petersburg. It was famous for fireworks and balloon rides which were offered there.[27] Thus, the allusions to the Aztecs elicit associations with small people who pose as someone far more lofty. Izler, on the other hand, brings to mind fireworks (man playing with fire) and an ascent into the sky. But the report about a woman's fall down the stairs suggests precisely the opposite – a precipitous descent. The stairs themselves inevitably bring to mind the stairway leading to the police station and the stairs on which Porokh beats the landlady in Raskol'nikov's dream. The notion of a fire is present in the report about the death of the merchant as well as the reports of housefires. ("Burn up" is a common term for death from sudden consumption of great quantities of alcohol.) The author certainly associated these housefires with Elijah the Prophet. Thus, the carefully organized sequence of headlines is more than a reflection of contemporary Petersburg realia. They subtly allude to Raskol'nikov's Napoleonic attempt to take the law of God and man into his own hands and to usurp the authority of Elijah. But the usurper's attempt to ascend into the heavenly heights fails, and he tumbles from the sky, scorched by the prophet's fire.[28]

After the storm, Raskol'nikov visits his mother and sister and goes to Sonia, where he "takes on the cross" by accepting a small cypress cross which she gives him. Then he kisses the ground at the crossroads and goes to "drink the cup," while Sonia follows. As in the first episode at the police station, the word "dukh" and its cognates suggest a spiritual significance in Raskol'nikov's final encounter with Porokh. Once again he stops to catch his breath (*perevesti dukh*) before entering the police station [406]. When he enters, Il'ia Petrovich greets him, exclaiming:

"Ah! 'He can't be seen, and he can't be heard, but...' How's it go in the fairytale?...'I smell a Russian'?... Can't remember!" [406]

The formula Porokh is trying to recall from Russian folktales is *russkim dukhom pakhnet,* which is comparable to "Fee, fie, fo, fum, I smell the blood of an Englishman!" It means 'I smell a Russian,' and is said of the Russian fairytale hero when he has become invisible but his presence is detected. However, because *dukh* means 'spirit' as well as 'odor,' the formula can be rendered literally as 'I smell a Russian spirit.' It is this symbolic, secondary meaning which is most significant. The contrite "Russian spirit" which Porokh now smells presents a neat contrast to the smell of the German brothel keeper's perfume (*dukhi*), which was so conspicuous in the first police station episode. Further repetition of the word *dukh* in the scene of the confession underscores its symbolic importance. Porokh uses it in characterizing Raskol'nikov: "...learned studies — that's where your spirit soars!" [407-8] Porokh also casually refers to the stuffiness of the police station: "The air [*dukh*] here is so stopped up..." [409], an authorial allusion to Raskol'nikov's entrapped spirit which yearns to be free from the fetters of the crime.

Near the end of each episode at the police station, Raskol'nikov is offered a glass of water. He faints after his first interview with Porokh and wakes up to "a yellow glass filled with yellow water" [83]. In the second police station episode, as Raskol'nikov confesses, Il'ia Petrovich offers him a glass of water and enjoins him to drink [409-10]. Both these drinking motifs, and especially the "yellow water," recall the "bitter cup" of suffering which Raskol'nikov resolves to drink when he ascends the spiral staircase to face "Elijah the Prophet." In neither case does he actually drink the water, but in confessing he accepts the "cup" of suffering. These drinking motifs derive ultimately from Matthew 27: 33-34:

> When they had reached a place called Golgotha, that is, the place of the skull, they gave him wine to drink mixed with gall, which he tasted but refused to drink.

Note that the Russian word for "yellow" (*zheltyi*) shares the same root with the word for "gall" (*zhelch'*).[29]

Svidrigailov also spends part of the night in the thunderstorm. But his entire life has been consumed by debauchery, and visions of his past torment him when he tries to sleep. For him the thunderstorm is an apocalyptic time of Judgment. Illuminated by Elijah's lightning, his transgressions become unbearable to him and he finally commits suicide.

While Raskol'nikov's path to suffering and resurrection resembles that of Christ, Svidrigailov follows the path of Judas, who accepted thirty pieces of silver for betraying Christ. Svidrigailov sells his soul to Marfa Petrovna for thirty thousand pieces of silver when she ransoms him from jail for thirty thousand silver rubles.[30] In Slavonic church writings, Judas is said to have hanged himself on a "bush" (*kust*). Dmitrii Karamazov considers following in Judas' path when, with the remnants of three thousand rubles in a bag under his shirt, he thinks of hanging himself on a bush (*rakita*, also known as *rakitov kust*) by the roadside.[31] Svidrigailov, too, contemplates suicide beneath a bush (*kust*) on one of the Petersburg islands [392, 394]. But he only walks as far as a police station on Vasil'evskii Island and, finding it equally suitable, he shoots himself as a *Jewish* fireman watches. (This building also served as a fire station; the fire department in Petersburg and other Russian cities was an agency of the police.)[32] The station has a watchtower which, in the context of the thunderstorm and other fiery-prophet motifs, suggests a divine presence, an "Overseer" who watches events from above. When Svidrigailov first sees the watchtower, he thinks: "At least there will be an official witness." [394] The station is symbolically equivalent to the office of Il'ia Porokh, emanation of Elijah.

On the eve of his suicide, Svidrigailov visits a beer garden where a gloomy German clown and some off-tune songsters are entertaining the public. When a quarrel erupts among some copyists (*pisarishki*: writers in caricature), they ask Svidrigailov to be their "judge." He "judges" them for fifteen minutes, but the only thing that is clear to him is that one of them has stolen a silver spoon from the eating establishment and pawned it off to a Jew.[33] Svidrigailov simply pays for the spoon himself and leaves. This little scandal involving a mere silver spoon mirrors his own Judas' path, much as the scandal at the German brothel keeper's (involving a hack writer) reflects Raskolnikov's crime. Svidrigailov's sitting in "judgment" over a petty thief is a parody of the divine Judgment before which Svidrigailov himself stands.

When he returns to his hotel that night, Svidrigailov hears in the next room a strange sort of whisper, sometimes bordering on a muffled shout. When he peers through a crack in the wall, he sees two men:

> One of them had removed his jacket. He had extremely curly hair and a red, inflamed face. He held the pose of an orator, with his feet wide apart in order to maintain his balance, and, pounding himself on the chest, he reproached the other man in pathetic tones, saying that he was a beggar with no rank, that he had pulled him up out of the mud, that he could drive him out if he wanted to, and that there was *only the finger of the Almighty to see them.* His friend sat there on the chair looking like someone who wants very much to sneeze, but can't. He cast an occasional dull, ram-like glance at the orator, but evidently had no comprehension of what he was talking about, and probably wasn't even listening. A candle was burning to the end on the table. There was also a nearly empty carafe of water, wine glasses, bread, cups, cucumbers and teacups that had long been empty. Surveying this scene, Svidrigailov walked away from the crack and sat down on his bed. [389]

The dull-witted "beggar" in this scene symbolizes Svidrigailov's fallen spirit. Turning this beggar back out (into the "mud") is a foreshadowing of Svidrigailov's death in the rain when his conscience can no longer bear Elijah's punishment. The upraised "finger of the Almighty" corresponds to the watchtower which rises over the police station like a church belltower.[34]

The police building which evidently served as the real prototype for Porfirii's office also has a watchtower on its roof.[35] In his game of cat-and-mouse with the murderer, Porfirii Petrovich employs various turns of speech which allude to Raskol'nikov's role as usurper of the prophet's fire. When Raskol'nikov only reacts cynically to his suggestion that he confess, Porfirii replies: "What sort of prophet are you?" [351] At one point he refers to himself as the target of a thunderbolt:

"...And do you remember Mikolka? Do you remember it well? Now that was thunder for you! A thunderbolt right out of the clouds! Yes, but how did I take it? I didn't believe that thunderbolt even a tiny bit, you saw for yourself!..." [347]

Thus, Porfirii recognizes this figurative "thunderbolt" to be false, and the passage is suggestive of a usurper-prophet (Raskol'nikov). The real thunder and lightning are on Porfirii's side. When Porfirii interviews Raskol'nikov in Part 5, thoughts flash in Raskol'nikov's mind "like lightning." Repetition of this image in one paragraph makes it conspicuous:

> "Yesterday, it seems, you said you would like to ask me... officially... about my acquaintance with the... the woman who was killed?" Raskol'nikov began again. Then the thought flashed in his mind *like lightning*: "Now why did I go and say 'it seems'?" Then immediately another thought flashed *like lightning*: "Now why am I so worried that I said 'it seems'?" [255]

Later in the same scene, after tormenting Raskol'nikov with his endless hints and insinuations, Porfirii notices that Raskol'nikov has turned pale and complains that the room is stifling (*dushno*). At this point, Raskol'nikov loses his temper and exclaims that he will not permit Porfirii to continue torturing him. Porfirii replies that Raskol'nikov is having an "attack" (*pripadok*, derived from *padat'* 'to fall')[36] and hands him a glass of water, urging him to drink [264]. As at the police station, Raskol'nikov refuses to drink. He raises the glass to his lips and sets it down with distaste. In the chatter which ensues, Porfirii exclaims "Lord!" three times and "for Christ's sake" once in a single paragraph [265]. Once again, the glass of water is linked symbolically with the cup of gall offered to Christ on the path to Golgotha. In its religious imagery, the episode at Porfirii's office mirrors the first scene at the police station. Like Il'ia Petrovich, Porfirii Petrovich is a symbolic emanation of Elijah the Prophet, the divine tormentor who brings sinners to Justice, although the connection is faintly drawn and barely discernible. In Part 6, after Porfirii insinuates that Raskol'nikov is trying to play the role of a prophet, Raskol'nikov exclaims:

> "... And what sort of prophet are you? From the heights of what majestic calm do you utter these all-wise prophecies?" [352]

Shortly thereafter, Porfirii speaks of the approaching storm, and Raskol'nikov leaves.

One might try to explain in purely psychological terms Raskol'nikov's final resolve to confess and "drink the cup". One might argue that his decision to go to Porokh is prompted by a masochistic impulse. But the world of *Crime and Punishment* reaches beyond the realm of body and mind alone, encompassing God and the human spirit. The symbolic Biblical motifs throughout the novel all point to a deeper awareness of sin and to a spiritual need to seek atonement through suffering.

A number of critics, including Konstantin Mochul'skii, claim that Raskol'nikov's spiritual transformation in the epilogue hardly follows from the earlier characterization of the hero.[37] According to Mochul'skii, the epilogue is a poorly contrived appendage to the novel, hastily concocted in order to please the readership and publisher.[38] However, the symbolism associated with Elijah both in the final version and in the drafts shows that the murderer's spiritual resurrection was envisioned by Dostoevsky long before the writing of the novel was nearing its end. Raskol'nikov's transformation is slow and gradual; even in the epilogue it has barely begun. Nevertheless, some will still claim, along with Mochul'skii, that such a turnabout seems unlikely in a character of Raskol'nikov's type. But who really knows? As one of the drafts states in what was foreseen as the final line of the novel: "Wondrous are the ways in which God will find a man."[39]

Part Two: *The Village of Stepanchikovo* and *The Possessed*

> *Meanwhile, for two weeks now Iliusha had hardly left his bed in the corner, beneath the icons.*
> — *The Brothers Karamazov*

As in the climactic chapter of *Crime and Punishment*, where Elijah's thunderstorm is of capital importance as a symbol of the divine presence which urges Raskol'nikov to confess, a violent thunderstorm culminates the action in *The Village of Stepanchikovo and Its Inhabitants* (1858-1859).[1] In this earlier novel, the storm occurs precisely on the feast day of Elijah, and the thunder and lightning are attributed explicitly to the wrathful prophet. Besides the insights it provides concerning Dostoevsky's allegorical technique and his use of folklore, *Stepanchikovo* is invaluable for the light it sheds on the final chapters of *The Possessed* (1870-72).[2] Here we shall examine the spiritual symbols of *Stepanchikovo*, including the climactic lightning storm, before turning to Stepan Trofimovich Verkhovenskii's path to salvation in *The Possessed*.

Stepanchikovo is a light, farcical portrayal of the confrontation between two contrasting personalities: Egor Il'ich Rostanev and Foma Fomich Opiskin. Rostanev is a forerunner of Prince Myshkin in *The Idiot*. He is naïve and childlike in the extreme. Meek and self-effacing, "he would give away his own shirt" or "carry someone for miles on his back" [5]. His hospitality has no limits, and his home becomes a refuge for spongers and poor relatives. Slandered and taken advantage of by those around him, Egor Il'ich nevertheless invents every imaginable excuse to justify the sins of others, all the time blaming and criticizing himself.

Foma Fomich, on the other hand, is a petty, vain, backbiting tyrant who tries to usurp all authority in

Rostanev's home, where he lives as the confidant (and possibly the clandestine lover) of Rostanev's mother. With hopes of improving their own fortunes, she and Foma try to coerce Rostanev into marrying the rather "touched" but wealthy spinster Tat'iana Ivanovna. An obstacle in their path is the young governess Nastas'ia, with whom Egor has fallen in love. However, his love for Nastas'ia is so unselfish and noble that he is even willing to marry the rich spinster in order to make everyone happy, if only Nastas'ia can remain in his house. In order to legitimize this arrangement in the eyes of his mother and other members of her camp, he enlists the aid of his nephew, inviting him from Petersburg to his country estate with the hope that the young man will want to marry Nastas'ia.

But the nephew soon perceives that the love between Nastas'ia and Rostanev is deep, sincere and mutual, and he is quick to see the absurdity and unfairness of the predicament which has been imposed upon his uncle. He is shocked and exasperated by the ways in which Foma tyrannizes and manipulates Rostanev, who acquiesces to Foma's every demand and virtually lives as a servant in his own home. A thoroughgoing xenophile, Foma even sets about reforming the servants and peasants by teaching them French and trying to frenchify their manners and habits.

When the young peasant boy Falalei repeatedly dreams of a white bull, Foma shames him for not dreaming of something more lofty and noble. He also forbids the boy to dance the Komarinsky, a national Russian dance which celebrates the exploits of a drunken peasant. But Falalei persists in dancing the Komarinsky, a temptation too strong for his poetic nature to resist, and the white bull keeps reappearing to him in his dreams no matter how hard he tries to stop it. The bull functions as a symbol of the rough-hewn peasantry – of the Russian nation in its actual, quintessential form, a culture with which Foma will not be reconciled. As the patron and representative of this culture, Rostanev is casually compared with a bull when Foma tells him: "You understand as much about the lofty and refined as a bull understands about beef!" [74] A parallel symbol is the name of Korovkin (derived from *korova* 'cow'), whom everyone expects to appear as Foma's opponent in a philosophical debate. But when he finally arrives at the end of the novel, he is drunk and covered with straw after sleeping in a barn! No philosophical debate takes place after all.

   The novel's climax comes on the holiday of Elijah the Prophet (July 20). Egor Il'ich gets up in the morning intending to propose on this day to Tat'iana Ivanovna in order to placate his mother and Foma. But his neighbor Bakhcheev arrives with news that the young man Obnoskin has carried off Tat'iana to marry her and, obviously, to become heir to her wealth. Flattered by the young man's attentions and tempted by the romantic dream of elopement which she has doubtless harbored throughout her adult life, she has willingly gone with Obnoskin. However, she soon has a change of heart and reaches out pleadingly to Bakhcheev as he passes their carriage while on his way to the holiday Mass at a nearby monastery. Instead of continuing on to church, Bakhcheev races to warn Rostanev of the abduction.

   A chase ensues, led by Rostanev and Bakhcheev, and the crazy spinster is rescued. Obnoskin attempts apologetically to explain his actions by stating that he intended to use his wealth in order to help the poor and to establish a stipend for needy students. Obnoskin's naïve, straightforward manner suggests that this was indeed a sincere motive, although it coexisted alongside his mother's goal of self-aggrandizement. Obnoskin's charitable aim (which, incidentally, parallels the altruistic goal behind Raskol'nikov's murder of the old pawnbroker), coupled with his mother's greed, serves as a moral mirror for Rostanev, who sees that he, too, was about to commit an unconscionable act in marrying Tat'iana. As in the case of Obnoskin, his own motives were unselfish and altruistic, even if misguided, while his mother's goals for inducing him to marry were self-seeking and reprehensible. Thus, Rostanev sees the error of his ways, although the necessity to marry Tat'iana Ivanovna has now fallen away of itself, as the fiasco of the elopement has cast a dark shadow on her sanity and respectability, virtually eliminating her as a potential bride for Rostanev.

The crisis of Tat'iana Ivanovna's abduction is only the prelude to the final disaster which ensues the same day. It is the nameday of Rostanev's eight-year-old son Iliusha (a form of endearment for *Il'ia* 'Elijah'). However, jealous of the attention which Iliusha will receive on his nameday, Foma has announced that his nameday falls on the same date. It is a blatant lie, but Iliusha nevertheless memorizes a mock epic poem by the farcical, fictitious poet Kuz'ma Prutkov and recites the poem in Foma's honor when all are assembled after the rescue of Tat'iana. But Foma is insulted by the undignified tone of the poem and announces that he is parting with Rostanev forever. He lambasts Egor Il'ich and proceeds to give hypocritical advice to everybody, as though he were a departing Savior.

Rostanev has yielded to Foma's tyranny and criticism throughout the novel, but his patience now suddenly comes to an end when Foma proceeds to slander Nastas'ia. Foma accuses her of an indecent liaison with Rostanev, claiming that Egor Il'ich has thoroughly corrupted her morals. At this point, Egor Il'ich takes Foma by the shoulders and flings him "like a straw" through glass doors leading outside. Foma flies through the closed doors and down seven steps into the yard. Following Rostanev's instructions, the servant Gavrila drives Foma away on a wagon. Inside, the women scream and nearly faint; Falalei sobs. The smashing of the doors is soon echoed by the crash of thunder as a powerful lightning storm begins outside:

> [...] I shall also add that at this minute a strong thunderstorm unleashed itself outside: the blows of the thunder could be heard more and more frequently, and the large drops of rain began to knock at the windows.
> "There's a nice holiday for you!" muttered Mr. Bakhcheev as he lowered his head and spread his fingers. [139]

Amid the pandemonium, Egor Il'ich asks Nastas'ia to marry him, but she and her impoverished father Evgraf try to dissuade him, arguing that she is too lowly and undignified for him. Evgraf then joins Rostanev's mother in urging him to go rescue Foma from the storm. Rostanev replies:

> "Wait a minute, Evgraf Larionich!" shouted Uncle Egor. "I beg you, listen to just one more word I have to say! *Just one more word...*"
> Having said this, he walked over to the corner, sat down in an armchair, lowered his head and covered his eyes with his hands, as though reflecting on something.
> At this moment, *a terrifying blow of thunder* crashed almost directly over the house. The whole building shook. Egor's mother screamed. So did Perepelitsyna. Other women in the room made the sign of the cross, dumb from fear. So did Bakhcheev.
> "*Lord, it's Elijah the Prophet!*" whispered five or six voices all at once.
> The thunder was followed by such a terrible downpour that *it seemed like an entire lake had been overturned* over Stepanchikovo.
> "What about Foma Fomich? What'll happen to

him out in the fields?" squeaked the old maid Perepelitsyna.
"Egorushka! Go bring him back!" his mother cried in despair. Then, as though insane, she lunged toward the door. The other women restrained her, flocking all around, sobbing, screaming and consoling her. It was *Sodom* at its worst!
"He left in just his jacket. If he at least had an overcoat!" continued Perepelitsyna. "And he didn't take an umbrella, either. The lightning will kill him!.." [142][3]

On a symbolic plane, the rage of Egor Il'ich is the wrath of the thundering Elijah. Egor's patronymic (*Il'ich* 'son of Elijah') and the name he has given his son (*Il'ia* 'Elijah'), therefore, are both replete with meaning. His officer's rank (*polkovnik* 'regimental commander'), like the officer's rank of Il'ia Porokh, is an additional link with the Biblical prophet who could destroy armies with divine fire and who later came to be seen as an armed enforcer of divine law.

Egor Il'ich seems to invoke the thunder as he meditates in the armchair. The thunder is his "one more word." The casual comparison of the downpour to an overturned lake is actually less casual than it appears at first glance. It ties in with one of Foma's tirades in which he chastises Rostanev for being cruel to his mother (a totally groundless accusation, of course):

> "How will you feel," Foma said, "if your own mother, the instigator, so to speak, of your very life, takes a walking stick in hand and actually goes begging, leaning on her stick and reaching out with withered, trembling hands? ...and at this very moment you'll be drowning somewhere in your feather mattress and... well, in luxury and so forth!

> It's horrible, simply horrible! But most horrible of all is the way you stand here in front of me like a dumb pillar, blinking your eyes and with your mouth all agaw. It's plain indecent! At the very suggestion of this actually happening you should be tearing out your hair by the roots and pouring out streams... what am I saying! – rivers, lakes, seas, oceans of tears!.." [10]

Although Foma is unaware of it, his words foreshadow the thunderstorm which accompanies Rostanev's wrathful explosion. The storm of Elijah is the storm of Egor Il'ich, who, like Il'ia Porokh, is an earthly manifestation of the prophet. While the "lakes" of tears correspond to the "lake" of rain which inundates Stepanchikovo, Egor's "tearing out his hair by the roots" evokes associations with Elijah's habit of uprooting trees. And, in this context, the allusion to Egor's "drowning" in a feather mattress brings to mind a heavenly deity lolling on the clouds.[4]

Rostanev bears an outward resemblance to the blustering but good-hearted Il'ia Porokh:

> He resembled the epic heroes of Russian folklore: tall and well-built, with ruddy cheeks and teeth as white as ivory. He had a long brown mustache and a loud, ringing voice. His laughter came in open-hearted volleys and he spoke jerkily in a clipping staccato. [5]

The "volleys" of Rostanev's laughter (*raskatistyi smekh*) correspond to the "volleys" of Elijah's thunder (*raskaty groma* [136]). The comparison of Rostanev to the heroes of the Russian folk epic is not fortuitous.[5] Dostoevsky doubtless has in mind Il'ia Muromets (Elijah of Murom), who is linked with Elijah the Prophet in the Russian oral tradition.[6] He alludes to Il'ia Muromets in the earlier novella *A Little Hero,* and in his later notebooks he repeatedly mentions Il'ia Muromets as the spiritual ideal of the Russian folk imagination.[7] Rostanev's throwing Foma through the closed doors recalls the fighting tactics of Il'ia Muromets, who pushes the heathen foe right through the wall of the Kiev palace.[8]

Rostanev embodies both the wrathful and merciful dimensions of Elijah the Prophet. After throwing Foma out into the storm, he finally consents to go rescue him if he will "publicly confess his guilt" and ask Nastas'ia's forgiveness. Egor mounts his horse Polkan and rides away bareback in search of Foma, whose wagon has already landed in a ditch when the horse was frightened by lightning. Rostanev finds Foma, who had set out on foot with his walking stick, but then headed back toward Stepanchikovo, afraid of the storm.[9] Some peasants in a wagon help bring Foma back to the house.

Foma remains an incorrigible hypocrite, but his tyranny is now tempered somewhat. He gives his blessing to Rostanev's marriage, praising Nastas'ia's purity of soul, thereby making everyone happy.

Soon thereafter, Rostanev discusses the problem of good and evil with his nephew. Their conversation can be seen as a statement of one of the novel's central themes (however poorly it is demonstrated on the example of Foma Fomich). The nephew remarks that "the depths of the human soul cannot be fathomed" and that one should not give up hope for those who have fallen morally [160-161].[10] In replying, Egor Il'ich speaks of the trees which have been washed clean by the storm:

> "[...] But just look what a fine spot this is!" he added, looking all around. "What nature! What a picture! And what a tree! Just look! As big around as a man! What sap, what leaves! And the sun! Look how everything has perked up and been washed clean after the storm... You'd think the trees also comprehend something about themselves,

that they feel and enjoy life..." [161]

The tree is clearly a symbol of man, his soul renewed by the Water of Life and his conscience illuminated by the divine lightning. The message is one of hope and faith in the divine spark which glows in every human soul.

This theme is conveyed most poignantly when Foma taunts and ridicules the simple peasant boy Falalei:

> "[...] Now what do you think? Can there possibly be even a piece or scrap of soul in this living hunk of beef? [...] Why are you standing there with your mouth ajar? Want to swallow a whale? Tell me: do you think you're beautiful [*prekrasen* implies 'noble,' 'magnificent']?"
> "Yes, I'm b-b-beautiful!" Falalei replied through muffled sobs. [66-67]

The same theme is echoed by the servant Gavrila when he finally lashes out against Foma for trying to humiliate him:

> "No, Foma Fomich," Gavrila replied with dignity. "I'm not being vulgar and it wouldn't be proper for me, a serf, to be vulgar in your presence, sir. But every man carries the image of God, His image and likeness. It's my sixty-third year, sir. [...] And never in my life have I seen anything as indecent as this!" [75]

An inner consciousness of his own spirituality gives the simple Russian peasant a resolute sense of dignity which even Foma cannot break.

But if all men bear the likeness of God in their souls, they also carry the potential to become like the Devil. These two spiritual polarities are manifested in the eccentric personalities of the all-forgiving Egor Il'ich and the vain, conniving Foma Fomich. Throughout the novel, the author hints at Rostanev's associations with Elijah and God, using the seemingly casual details and turns of speech that are typical of his style. Rostanev's home, for example, is said to be a "Noah's ark" [6] for all the poor friends and relatives who find refuge there. The allusion is to God's mercy, reflected in Egor Il'ich, and the promise of salvation.[11]

When the peasants in Rostanev's village of Kapitonovka hear the false rumor that he is planning to consign sixty-eight *souls* (i.e. serfs) over to Foma, they appear before Egor Il'ich praying for mercy (*otmolit'sia*):

> "[...] they've taken it into their heads that I'm going to give them away, all of Kapitonovka... sixty-eight souls to Foma Fomich!"
> "We don't want anybody except you!" the peasants intoned all at once like a choir. "You're the father and we're the children!"

The underlying image is unmistakable: it is the flocks of the faithful invoking God Himself.

> "[...] and always come to me when you have need; come straight to me any time!"
> "Our father! You are the father and we are the children! Please don't forsake us for Foma Fomich!" [34]

> "[...] Walk with God now and I'll be happy... don't worry now, I won't abandon you."
> "Defend us, Father!"
> "Let us see your light, Father!"
> And the peasants all fell down at his feet.
> "Come on now, this is nonsense! Bow down to God and the Czar, not to me... Go on now. Conduct yourselves well and you'll earn kindness [*zasluzhite lasku*]..." [36]

In similar fashion, the word *gospodin* ('master,' 'lord') is carefully manipulated to point to Rostanev's symbolic identification with God. Several examples could be cited, but most interesting is the episode in which Egor Il'ich finally relieves Gavrila of the unbearable burden of trying to learn French:

> "[...] What are you doing with that French lesson book?" he yelled wrathfully [*s iarost'iu*], turning to Gavrila. "Away with it! Burn it! Trample it! Tear it up! *I* am your lord and master and *I'm* telling you to stop trying to learn French. You must obey me because *I* am your lord and master, not Foma Fomich!.."
> "Praise Thee, O Lord!" Gavrila mumbled quietly. [81]

Among the other multifarious turns of speech that are used in this way, one might single out the nephew's promise to be ready to help Rostanev "forever and ever" (*vo veki vekov*) [81]. This scriptural, prayer-like formula is echoed later in the same chapter when Egor swears "by all the saints" that he is Foma's friend "forever and ever." Repeated allusions to "paradise" and casual reference to Nastas'ia and other characters as "angels" again seem to identify Rostanev with God, enthroned and surrounded by the saints and angels.[12]

The old valet Gavrila is appropriately named after the Archangel Gabriel, who in church lore is traditionally portrayed at the side of the Divinity. Rostanev's sister Praskov'ia is named after St. Paraskeva "Piatnitsa," who commonly appears alongside St. Anastasia and Elijah in icon art.[13] The icon of Paraskeva was carried in ritual processions on Elijah's feast day in some regions.[14] She is a spiritual "sister" of Elijah not only in the broad sense (i.e. as a fellow saint), but also in that she, too, struggled against idolatry.[15] Her name is the Greek word meaning

'Friday;' hence, her Russian epithet *Piatnitsa* 'Friday.' Her cult was popular throughout Russia, where she was seen as a patron of women and of household activities such as spinning, weaving and sewing.[16] She never married, devoting her life to God, and a number of convents in Russia bear her name. Afanas'ev links her cult with a pre-Christian deity corresponding to the Germanic goddess Freya, whose day of provenance was Friday.[17] The thunder god Thor (and possibly his Slavic cousin Perun, the forerunner of Elijah) was associated with Thursday.[18] Thus, here is another sense in which Paraskeva might be viewed as a "sister" of Elijah.

Dostoevsky hints at the connection between Praskov'ia and Paraskeva, the patron of women, in Bakhcheev's characterization of Praskov'ia:

> "[...] I have no desire to even speak of Egor Il'ich's sister Praskov'ia Il'inichna. Forty years old and she's still unmarried. Nothing but oo's and ah's, and cackles like a hen. I've had all of it I can take. All there is to her is just her female sex. That's all there is to respect in her – nothing but the fact that she's of the female sex. [...]" [24]

In the final chapter, which serves as an epilog, one learns that Bakhcheev eventually proposed marriage to Praskov'ia, but was refused. Instead, she devotes her life to her brother and Nastas'ia:

> [...] Praskov'ia Il'inichna lives with them and takes pleasure in serving and pleasing them in every way. It is she who looks after the household tasks. Mr. Bakhcheev proposed to her soon after Uncle's wedding, but she gave him a flat refusal. Everyone then concluded that she would enter a convent, but that didn't happen either. Praskov'ia Il'inichna has one remarkable peculiarity: she totally effaces

herself before those whom she loves, constantly disappears from their view, looks them in the eyes, submits to all their caprices, looks after them and serves them. Now, after the death of her mother, she considers it her duty to stay by her brother's side and to serve [*ugozhdat'*] Nastas'ia in every possible way. [166]

The epithets applied to Praskov'ia throughout the novel – "good," "humble," "compassionate" – all serve to highlight her saintly qualities.

The name of Rostanev's meek and humble bride is derived from Greek *Anastasia* 'Resurrection'. As noted above, St. Anastasia is commonly portrayed alongside Elijah and St. Paraskeva in Russian icons.[19] While Rostanev's patronymic is associated with Elijah the Prophet, his first name, Egor, is a folk variant of Georgii, from St. George. Appropriately for Rostanev, this saint is viewed as a benevolent patron of the peasant farmer.[20]

Thus, the portrait of Rostanev, Praskov'ia and Nastas'ia is that of man in the likeness of God and His saints. Fallen man, or man in the likeness of the Devil, is best represented by Foma, whose last name, *Opiskin*, (from *opiska* 'a slip of the pen') is suggestive of imperfection and the notion of sin, or moral error.[21] "Thrice-accursed," "anathema," "serpent-monster" (*ekhidna*): these epithets, commonly applied to the Devil, are applied to Foma, quite aptly, by characters in the novel. Foma's hypocrisy is entirely transparent, so it is easy for the reader to simply invert the meaning of his words to arrive at the truth. For example, when Foma declares that he is leaving Stepanchikovo forever, he says that he is "enriched with new knowledge about the corrupt condition of the human race." [137] He means to condemn Egor Il'ich, but the author is clearly alluding to Foma's own fallen state.

Similarly, when Foma speaks of Rostanev's "serpent

speeches" (*zmeinye rechi* [85]), it is clear that the allusion is to Foma as serpent-Devil. He has seduced Rostanev's mother – "the female half" of the household – with his pseudoscience and false erudition – in short, with his Tree of Knowledge. He formerly served as a "jester" (*shut* – also a term for the Devil) for her husband until his death and was adept at mimicking all sorts of animals. This motif is intended to evoke associations with the animal metamorphoses of the Devil, which abound in Christian lore.[22] The narrator uses figures of speech which are evocative of serpents and black magic in his characterization of Foma:

> [...] he could sometimes foretell the future, but he was especially good at interpreting dreams and he was a master at condemning his neighbor. [8]
>
> Foma Fomich is the personification of the most boundless vanity, but of a particular kind of vanity: the kind that afflicts complete nonentities and, as usual in such cases, it is the vanity of one who has been injured and downtrodden by painful failures; it is vanity which has been festering for a long, long time and which secretes envy and venom at any encounter, at anyone else's success. [11]

Hearing of Foma's antics, "good people would make the sign of the cross and spit" [13], a common folk form of simple exorcism.

The ejection of Foma from Rostanev's home elicits associations with Satan's expulsion from heaven. The seven porch steps down which Foma falls seem to correspond to the seven heavens. But it is also reminiscent of the exile of Adam and Eve from the Garden of Eden and of the Last Judgment. Foma's falling down the porch steps (which he later refers to as "my fall") is evocative of man's fall from grace. In both *Crime and Punishment* and *The Idiot*, the motif of falling down the stairs is endowed with the same symbolism of the fall into sin.[23]

As a symbol of the wrath of God, the lightning of Elijah is closely linked with the apocalyptic "cup of God's wrath" and with the "grapes of wrath" which are reaped in the Apocalypse. Egor speaks of this cup after he has thrown out Foma, while the storm still rages:

> "Momma!" he continued. "The cup was full to overflowing. You saw for yourself. That's not the way I wanted things to happen, but the hour struck and it had to be done!" [140]

As the storm first gathers overhead, Foma, too, unaware of the apocalyptic implications of his speech, talks arrogantly about reaping the hay:

> "And now a few details. They may be small, but they're indispensable, Egor Il'ich. The hay is still not mowed in the Khariinsky Meadow.[24] Don't wait till it's too late. Mow it, and mow it now! That's my advice..." [138]

Foma then advises Egor not to destroy the trees, and adds:

> "... It's too bad you sowed the *iarovóe* so late. It's amazing how late you sowed the *iarovóe*!.." [138]

Iarovóe refers to various grains sowed in the spring, but it is derived from *iaryi*, which most commonly means 'fierce,' 'wrathful.' *Iarost'* is one of the Biblical terms for God's wrath.[25] The sowing of the *iarovóe* is an allusion to the sowing and reaping of God's wrath. Once again, Foma's words are true in a way he never intends: it is indeed amazing how long it takes for Rostanev's wrath to reach fruition!

The scene of pandemonium which follows Rostanev's

explosion is referred to in a passage cited above as "Sodom at its worst" in order to highlight the associations with an apocalyptic cataclysm. Bakhcheev alludes figuratively to the Last Judgment when he first describes Foma's tyranny to the narrator:

> "... Yes, sir, I can tell you things that'll make your jaw fall open and you'll stand there with your mouth all agape until the Second Coming!" [25]

The theme of apocalyptic retribution is foreshadowed in the introductory chapter, where the nephew relates how once as a boy he and his uncle tied a mean old lady's house cap to a kite and launched it into the sky. The Russian word meaning 'kite' (*zmei*) also means 'dragon'. Thus, the boy and his uncle symbolically fed the evil woman to the dragon of the Apocalypse.

Strong overtones of blasphemy are present in Obnoskin's attempt to carry off Tatiana Ivanovna as well as in Foma's behavior at the nameday celebration. After all, their antics disrupt a religious holiday, the feast day of Elijah. The narrator notes that only Nastas'ia and Rostanev's children manage to attend church that day. Bakhcheev, whose trek to church was interrupted by the abduction attempt, grumbles during the chase: "They won't even let a man pray on God's holiday!" Later, when Rostanev ejects Foma to the accompaniment of thunder and lightning, Bakhcheev continues to mourn for the ruined church festival: "There's a fine holiday for you!" [139]

Foma is a usurper, like Satan, who would be supreme in heaven; Foma would rule the household, usurping the fire of Egor Il'ich, the symbolic Elijah. Fire imagery is repeatedly applied to him as he "burns," "flames" and "explodes" with envy and all his evil passions.[26] And yet, he hypocritically instructs Egor to extinguish the "housefire" of *his* unbridled passions:

"[...] if there is at least a spark of morality left in your heart, then bridle your passions! And if the destructive venom hasn't yet enveloped the whole building, then put out the housefire as best you can." [137]

By inverting the sense of Foma's words once again, one can decode the author's intended message: it is time for Elijah to extinguish the housefire of *Foma's* unbridled passions. The passage is another allusion to the rainstorm of Elijah.

The pleophonic, folk variant of the word for 'lightning' is consistently used instead of the standard literary form: *molon'ia* instead of *molniia*. Of course, it is intended to lend the dialog a colloquial flavor, but it also serves as a key to allegory in the novel. While the peasant boy Falalei is being persecuted by Foma for dreaming about the white bull, he grows thin and weak. In a vain ritual of exorcism, the chambermaid Malan'ia stands in the corner beneath the icons and sprinkles Falalei with sanctified water. Her name, *Malan'ia*, is chosen for its similarity to *molon'ia* ('lightning') in order to present the ritualistic sprinkling as a mild, symbolic storm of Elijah. Praskov'ia, a "living icon" of sorts, also participates in the ritual. One finds a similar association between the name *Malan'ia* and lightning in a fairytale about Czar Fire and Czaritsa Lightning (*Molniia* or *Malan'ia* in the various recordings).[27] Curiously, Bakhcheev's servant mentions a fairytale teller named Malan'ia when Rostanev's nephew first encounters them on the road to Stepanchikovo [21].[28]

As the Elijah motifs illustrate, Dostoevsky put great energy into *Stepanchikovo*. He considered it his best effort and waited impatiently to learn the opinions of editors and readers.[29] He must have been bitterly disappointed when most of the reviews proved to be negative. Nekrasov is said to have remarked: "Dostoevsky is washed up."[30] Pleshcheev's letter to A.P. Miliukov concerning the novel is especially interesting:

> "[...] Except for Rostanev (the uncle) there's not a single living character. It's all contrived and concocted; terribly clumsy. Please don't tell him this. I'll somehow avoid talking about it. It's a touchy business discussing this sort of thing. It could possibly harm our friendship. And, anyway, what sort of judge am I? Maybe the novel is superb and I simply don't understand it. I don't want to force my opinion on anyone. I haven't heard anyone else's reaction."[31]

Like Pleshcheev, various reviewers criticized *Stepanchikovo* for its lack of realism and contrived melodrama.[32] The novel certainly has its drawbacks. For example, as in much of Dostoevsky's fiction, much of the text seems unnecessarily long-winded. Nevertheless, a work should be judged according to the laws of its genre. *Stepanchikovo* is a farcical allegory, not a specimen of sheer realism. Before criticizing *Stepanchikovo* for not having "a single living character," one should first determine to what extent the characters are intended to be "true-to-life" human beings, as opposed to sacred images borrowed from the icon case.

In *The Possessed*, character portrayal and the narration of events are more intricate, creating at least the illusion of greater realism. But one still finds many of the same symbolic details and motif patterns which thread the text of *Stepanchikovo*. Once again, these symbolic motifs are clustered densely at the novel's climax, and a central symbol in the pattern is a rainstorm that is associated with a symbolic Elijah.

The dramatic events which culminate the novel's central action include a fire (which destroys an entire section of town), the murder of Shatov, the death of Liza Tushina, the elder Verkhovenskii's delirious pilgrimage, and Stavrogin's suicide. (The usual humdrum events so typical of life in a provincial Russian town...) On the morning before the fire, about seventy workers from a local factory assemble peacefully in front of the provincial governor's house in order to appeal to him for help in securing pay that is owed them by the factory management. The narrator explains that their intention is "to fall to their knees and to cry out, as though to Providence itself" when the governor appears. "The Russian nation," the narrator remarks, "has always loved a talk with 'the general himself'." [335-36] Soon the police arrive, led by the police chief Il'ia Il'ich ('Elijah the son of Elijah'). The narrator notes that Il'ia Il'ich enjoys "flying around" on his troika:

> It's total nonsense that he came flying on his troika at full speed and began fighting even before getting down. Often he did actually fly around. And he loved to fly around in his buggy with the little yellow rear end. And as his horses went out of their minds more and more as they were led to the point of debauchery, all the merchants on Merchants' Row would be in rapture, and Il'ia Il'ich would rise in his buggy, stand up straight, holding on to a sidestrap made specially for that purpose and, stretching his arm out into space like a monument, he would survey the whole town. [336][33]

This portrayal of the police chief as he "flies" in his buggy is patterned after the image of Elijah as he rises into the heavens on the fiery chariot. Icons usually show him standing in the chariot. Often one arm is reaching outward as he flies. The little *yellow* rear end of Il'ia's buggy is perhaps suggestive of fire.[34]

When he arrives at the governor's house, Il'ia "gets all heated up" and announces to the petitioners that "none of them will get off scot free." [337] Translated literally, the

Russian phrase means "nobody will emerge dry from the water." This statement engenders a rumor that the factory workers were sprayed with water from fire barrels at Il'ia's orders. Thus associated with a fire, the workers' demonstration foreshadows the fateful conflagration which is set by arsonists that night. Il'ia Il'ich interprets the demonstration as an act of insurrection. He is wrong, but the arson which comes later can be viewed as the attempt of nihilists to usurp the fire of this figurative Elijah.

The fire, of course, is in one way or another the handiwork of Petr Verkhovenskii, who has acted with the tacit complicity of Stavrogin. Their role as usurpers of Elijah's fire is intimated when Petr Verkhovenskii tries to persuade Stavrogin to become the secret leader of his underground organization. In describing the role of enigmatic leader which he envisions for Stavrogin, Petr Verkhovenskii casts him as Ivan Czarevich, the beloved, ever-victorious hero of fairytales. He also compares him to a new Elijah on a chariot of fire:

> "[...] Listen, I won't show you to anybody, not a soul. That's the best way. He exists, but nobody's seen him because he remains concealed. But then again, we could show you – say, to one in a hundred thousand. And word will go out all over the world: 'They've seen him! They've seen him!' Just like they saw the God Ivan Filippovich, Sabaoth,[35] ascend into heaven on his chariot. They saw him with their very own eyes! [...]" [326]

The terrorism of Petr's nihilists is portrayed as the inevitable fruit of the elder Verkhovenskii's liberal freethinking. As the climactic fire still burns, Stepan Trofimovich Verkhovenskii falls to his knees and confesses that he, too, has tried to usurp the divine fire:

> "[...] I bow down on my knees before all that was

beautiful and noble in my life! I kiss it and thank it all! Now I've split myself in two: behind me is a madman who dreamed of ascending into the heavens, *vingt deux ans*! But here stands a freezing, broken old man – a mere tutor *chez ce marchand, s'il existe pourtant ce marchand*..." [412]

    The symbolic Elijah, the police and fire chief Il'ia Il'ich, oversees the firemen's battle with the flames. The fire burns all night, but early in the morning it begins to rain. It is not the spectacular thunderstorm of *Crime and Punishment* or *Stepanchikovo*. After all, the month is November. But, coming to the aid of Il'ia's firefighters, the rain should certainly be attributed to the rainmaker Elijah. As the firemen fight to quell the fire of the nihilist usurpers, the fateful rendezvous takes place between Stavrogin and Liza Tushina, whose last name elicits associations with the verb *tushit'* ('to extinguish'). That night, Liza sees that the flame which burns in Stavrogin is not the pure flame of innocent love, but a cool, corrupt flame which will hardly burst into deeds of self-sacrifice. Stavrogin, too, comes to this realization and the experience can be said to "extinguish" all fire that remains within him.

    Stepan Trofimovich sets out in the rain to leave the town forever. It is a characteristically ridiculous but noble gesture symbolizing Stepan's repudiation of his former life, his atheism and his Western outlook. It is a pilgrimage in search of brotherly love, the true Russia and Christ.

    As a character type, Stepan closely resembles Foma Fomich Opiskin. His most prominent traits, including hysteria, effeminateness and gallomania, are shared by Foma. He, too, is a hanger-on who lives at the expense of his flighty confidante. Like Foma, he has tried to write fiction, managing only to write bizarre trash. Stepan Trofimovich lacks only the blatantly Mephistophelean features of Foma. (These traits were allotted to his son Petr.) In light of these similarities in character, Stepan's pilgrimage in the rain is strikingly reminiscent of Foma's exile during the thunderstorm. The mildness of the rain in *The Possessed* is more suggestive of the merciful aspect of Elijah as dispenser of the redeeming Water of Life.

Foma is rescued by the symbolic Elijah, Rostanev, and driven back to the house in a peasant wagon; Stepan Trofimovich is given a ride in a wagon by a red-bearded peasant and his wife. Before climbing into the wagon, Stepan thinks:

> "[...] It's strange... It's as though I were guilty before them, but I'm not guilty of anything before them." [483]

The narrator alludes to the "whirlwind" of Stepan's thoughts as the peasants help him into the wagon. Stepan has no clear idea where he wants to go, but the peasants conclude that the town of Spasov is his destination:

> "If you're a teacher, then why are you headed for Khatovo? Or are you going further?"
> "I... well, not exactly further... *C'est a dire*, I'm going to a certain merchant."
> "To Spasov, then?"
> "Yes, that's right. To Spasov. But then, it's all the same."
> "If you're going to Spasov on foot, it'll take you a week in those boots," the peasant woman laughed. [487]

Spasov is derived from *Spas* ('the Savior'). Hence, Stepan's pilgrimage is a journey to Salvation. He hopes to find work as a tutor in the home of some merchant, but on the allegorical level the "certain merchant" (*kupets*) he seeks is the Redeemer (*Iskupitel'*), derived from *kupit'* ('to buy'). In addition to this linguistic basis, the symbolic function of the merchant has scriptural associations as well. Most noteworthy is Matthew 13:45-46, which compares God to "a merchant who seeks fine pearls." Stepan's words, cited above, *ce marchand, s'il existe* reflects on the symbolic level Stepan's lack of faith in the God whom he seeks. (The merchants on Merchants' Row are in rapture when they see Il'ia Il'ich flying about on his troika, just as God might rejoice at the sight of his prophet as he wheels his way across the clouds in his chariot.)

Stepan and the peasants stop at a hut where they are served pancakes. Stepan asks for some vodka, using his habitual French:

> "How rich and tasty this is! If it's possible, may I have *un doigt d'eau de vie* ?" [485]

The symbolic allusion, of course, is to the Water of Life. He meets the wandering gospel vendor Sof'ia Matveevna, who joins him as he resumes his journey to Spasov. In a fever that is both physical and spiritual, Stepan speaks passionately of forgiveness:

> "Oh, we must forgive, we must forgive. Above all, we must forgive everyone and always. Let us hope that they will forgive us as well. Yes, because each and every one of us is guilty before the others. We're all guilty!" [491]

Then, as they ride further, Stepan's head begins to whirl and he drifts into a feverish sleep. He dreams of gaping jaws with terrifying teeth as they approach *Ust'evo*, derived from *ust'e* [and *ust-*] ('mouth'). In Ust'evo they hope to board the steamer which will take them to Spasov. Ust'evo is a symbolic place of Judgment for Stepan. As they wait in an inn for the steamer, Sof'ia tells him of the "woe" one endures in Ust'evo and about the stern innkeeper. "Terrible mythological lithographs" and icons adorn their room. Stepan "suffers" and is "tortured" by Sof'ia's warning that the stern master of the inn might charge an exorbitant sum for their room and meals. Here the allegory is developed further: the innmaster, like the merchant, symbolizes God. The exorbitant price represents the faith that is necessary for salvation. A casual allusion to God in Stepan's speech hints at the religious allegory: "*nous avons notre argent, et apres – et apres le bon Dieu.*" [493] The immediate meaning intended by Stepan is: "We have our money and afterwards the good Lord will help." But the literal meaning, which points to the allegory, is: "We have our money, and afterwards the good Lord"; i.e. "We'll pay with the faith that we have, and [hopefully] we'll enter the Kingdom of Heaven."[36]

Sof'ia tells Stepan that the proud, haughty master of the inn is a wealthy fisherman. "His net alone is worth a thousand rubles." [493] God as the Fisherman who catches men's souls in his net is an image which can be traced to the same source as the God-Merchant metaphor, Matthew 13:

> 45 "Again, the Kingdom of Heaven is like a merchant in search of fine pearls,
> 46 who, on finding one pearl of great value, went and sold all that he had and bought it.
> 47 "Again, the Kingdom of Heaven is like a net which was thrown into the sea and gathered fish of every kind;
> 48 when it was full, men drew it ashore and sat down and sorted the good into vessels but threw away the bad.
> 49 So it will be at the close of the age. The angels will come out and separate the evil from the righteous,
> 50 and throw them into the furnace of fire; there

men will weep and gnash their teeth.

The theme of spiritual "wealth" and the "price" one must pay for Redemption is continued in Sof'ia's reading from Chapter Three of the Apocalypse. The passage she reads also speaks of the divine "mouth," highlighting the role of Ust'evo as a place of Judgment:

> 14 "And to the angel of the church in Laodicea write: 'The words of the Amen, the faithful and true witness, the beginning of God's creation.
> 15 "'I know your works: you are neither cold nor hot. Would that you were cold or hot!
> 16 So, because you are lukewarm, and neither cold nor hot, I will spew you out of my mouth.
> 17 For you say, I am rich, I have prospered, and I need nothing; not knowing that you are wretched, pitiable, poor, blind, naked. [...]'"

When Varvara Petrovna learns that Stepan has set out for Spasov, she has four horses hitched to her carriage and races away along Stepan's "hot traces" to Ust'evo. When she first arrives, she storms and "thunders" about, jealous of Sof'ia Matveevna. But when she sees that Stepan is deathly ill, she looks after him, sending for a doctor and later urging him to accept final communion. At this point, however, Stepan needs no urging, having already undergone a spiritual transformation. Three days later he dies. When Varvara Petrovna declares that she will join Sof'ia in selling the gospel because she is now alone in the world, the doctor protests that she still has her son. The chapter ends with her reply:

> "I have no son!" Varvara Petrovna snapped. And as it turned out, it was as though she brought it on with her prophecy [*slovno naprorochila*]. [507]

Stavrogin chooses the highest little attic room in the house to hang himself. A long, narrow, "horribly steep" [*uzhasno krutoi*] stairway leads up to it. The Russian word meaning 'steep' (*krutoi*) is formed from the same root as the verb *krutit'* ('to twist; to whirl'). Hence, the steep stairway is remotely suggestive of a twisting stairway like that which Raskol'nikov climbs to reach the police station. The implied message is that Ivan Czarevich has ascended – into oblivion, rather like Svidrigailov by the firemen's watchtower.

Part Three: "Mr. Prokharchin"

And the Devil smote Job's children and his cattle and swept away his wealth, all at once, as though with God's thunder...
— Father Zosima

Dostoevsky's symbolic Elijah the Prophet in *Crime and Punishment* and *Stepanchikovo* can be traced back to the early story "Mr. Prokharchin," written in the spring and summer of 1846.[1] This curious tale was not received well by contemporary critics, including Belinsky.[2] Dostoevsky himself stated that work on the story proceeded slowly and without inspiration.[3] Overshadowed by the later novels and by works with clearer literary antecedents such as "The Double," "Mr. Prokharchin" has been neglected and inadequately appreciated in literary studies of Dostoevsky's *oeuvre*. However, subtle allegory, word play and literary allusions nevertheless make this story a delight for the careful reader. It attests to striking consistency in poetic technique over a wide span of years and belies the notion that an ideological gulf separates Dostoevsky's early works from those written after his return from Siberia.[4]

In addition to a policeman who figures as a symbolic Elijah, one finds in "Mr. Prokharchin" a landlady who is closely associated symbolically with the hero's conscience; apocalyptic allusions to the Last Judgment; and a housefire that is symbolic of divine retribution – motifs that were to resurface nineteen years later in the writing of *Crime and Punishment*. Woven into the apocalyptic allegory are clever allusions to Alexander Pushkin's "The Queen of Spades" (1834), a classic tale which also left a clear imprint on *Crime and Punishment*.[5] Here we shall examine the chain of apocalyptic allusions before turning to the Pushkinian motifs.

The idea for "Mr. Prokharchin" was likely suggested to Dostoevsky by press accounts of large sums of money found in the possession of apparent paupers after their death. For example, in June 1844, *The Northern Bee* reported the death of a civil servant who had lived in a tiny room on Vasil'evskii Island, subsisting mostly on bread and water. His landlady found over 1000 silver rubles in his mattress when he died from causes resembling malnutrition.[6] Dostoevsky's Semyon Ivanovich Prokharchin is a lowly civil servant who rents a small corner in a boarding house, drinking cheap herbs instead of tea and skimping on food in order to save a few kopeks. He pays less for his corner than other tenants and he constantly reminds his fellow lodgers that he is a poor man, alluding to his poor sister-in-law in Tver whom he helps to support. Actually, though, Prokharchin is a thoroughgoing misanthrope. He has neither imagination nor concern for his fellow man, and his "sister-in-law" is a myth which he has concocted as a smokescreen for nearly 2500 rubles horded away in his mattress.

Prokharchin is reticent and unsociable, and these qualities, together with his total lack of imagination, win him the disfavor of his fellow roomers. A trunk under his bed is filled with rags, old boots and worthless junk, but he keeps it carefully locked and even buys a special German lock – all as a ruse to distract attention from his mattress. When one of the young lodgers, Zinovii Prokof'evich, teases Prokharchin by suggesting that the chest might be the hiding place for a large fortune, the old miser reacts with unexpected violence. His goal to amass wealth is an *idée fixe* that has taken possession of his entire being. Zinovii's joke threatens to encroach upon this innermost secret of Prokharchin's soul. The demented old miser broods over the joke for several days and lashes out at Zinovii at every opportunity.

Then the boarders play a practical joke on Prokharchin. In his presence, they discuss a fictitious scheme to train and examine civil servants in the social graces. They hint at Prokharchin's antisocial behavior as they speak of the aims of the plan:

> "[...] people will dance and, in addition to all the earmarks of nobility, they will acquire polite behavior, courtesy, respect for their elders, a strong character, a good, open heart and all kinds of pleasant manners." [245]

This trauma and similar practical jokes affect the miser so deeply that one day he simply disappears. Three days later, the landlady sends the lodgers out in search of the "fugitive" with instructions to find him "dead or alive."

The lodger Sud'bin finds Prokharchin near a fleamarket and follows him to the scene of a housefire nearby. Prokharchin's fate is stalking him at this point, as suggested by the name *Sud'bin*, derived from *sud'ba* ('fate').[7] At the fire, Prokharchin is met by Zimoveikin, a drunken thief, vagrant and former bribe-taker whose name elicits associations with *zmei* ('dragon'). As further details show, he is symbolic of the Devil. The narrator relates how Zimoveikin tried to seduce the landlady and then directly proceeds to characterize him as Prokharchin's "seducer" (*obol'stitel'*):

> The next day everything ended quite lamentably. Either because Zimoveikin's characteristic dance proved to be all too characteristic or because he "shamed and disgraced" Ustin'ia Fedorovna, as she put it, "while she's a friend of Iaroslav Il'ich, and if she had wanted, she could have become an ober-officer's wife long ago" – whatever the reason, Zimoveikin was obliged to beat a hasty retreat. He left, then returned and was driven away ignominiously. Then he wedged his way into Semyon Ivanovich's good graces, relieving him of

his new slacks in the process, and now he made an appearance once again as Semyon Ivanovich's seducer. [247]

This sequence of "seductions" points to a symbolic connection between Prokharchin and his landlady. As in *Crime and Punishment*, she represents his conscience, or spiritual "mistress" (*khoziaika* 'landlady'; 'mistress of a household'). She is a friend of the policeman Iaroslav Il'ich, a symbolic Elijah the Prophet whose first name is derived from *iaryi* ('fierce') and whose patronymic means 'the son of Elijah.' Hence, he is the "fierce son of Elijah," a figurative descendant of the fiery prophet. Regardless who the landlady is referring to when she speaks of an *ober-officer*, her mentioning this rank together with Iaroslav Il'ich hints at Elijah's celestial sphere of activity, like the terms *nadziratel'* ('overseer,' 'superintendent') and *pomoshchnik nadziratelia* ('assistant to the superintendent'), which refer to Nikodim Fomich and Il'ia Porokh in *Crime and Punishment*. Thus, on an allegorical level Prokharchin's conscience, or "spiritual mistress," is acquainted with a symbolic Elijah, the enforcer of divine justice.

Like Raskol'nikov, Prokharchin owes a debt to his "spiritual mistress," whom he has deceived for years in paying a pauper's rent. On the symbolic plane, Zimoveikin alludes to this debt when he bows to the floor like a jester and rambles about gratitude and duty:

"...Senia, you're a nice man, congenial, not quick to take offence! You're straightforward, with good intentions... Do you hear? It's all because you're well-meaning. I'm the silly troublemaker, the panhandler. But you good people haven't abandoned me, I hope. I'm deeply honored. My thanks to all of you and to your landlady! You see, I bow to the ground. You see? There! My debt. I pay my debt, my dear landlady!" [256]

Although Zimoveikin contrasts himself with Prokharchin, whom he characterizes as a "doer of good deeds," his buffoonery actually mimics the miser's hypocritical pose as he pretends to be paying the landlady her due. After Prokharchin's death, Iaroslav Il'ich tells the landlady how to file for payment of the debt (*dolzhishek*). Symbolically, it represents the debt of conscience owed by a man who has no good deeds to his credit.

The spectacle of the housefire is a vision of the Last Judgment for the miser. He is brought home in a state of semi-consciousness at four o'clock in the morning. Later, as he lies in a fever, the fire is brought back to Prokharchin in a nightmarish delirium. He dreams that it is payday and he has just received his wages. As he descends the office stairway, he hides half the money in his boot, already inventing excuses for his presumed poverty which he can bring into play after paying the landlady her meager rent. In preparation for the vision of hellfire which is to follow, the term *zakonnoe vozmezdie* ('lawful retribution') is used for Prokharchin's wages.

On the stairway, Prokharchin encounters another office worker, Andrei Efimovich, a little bald man who alludes to his seven children as he counts his wages. "If there's no money, there'll be no kasha," he points out. He directs an angry glance at Prokharchin, as though Prokharchin were to blame for his seven children. Although the miser is "sure of his innocence, [...] "it nevertheless turns out that he, Semyon Ivanovich, is guilty." He suddenly fears that Andrei Efimovich will seize him and take away his "retribution," denying the existence of Prokharchin's sister-in-law and using the money for his seven children.

Prokharchin flees in panic, gasping for breath as he runs. Soon he is joined by a large crowd, who also run alongside him. Each jingles his own "retribution" in his back pocket as he runs. Like the trumpets of the Apocalypse, firemen's trumpets thunder as Prokharchin is swept by the waves of humanity to the scene of the fire. Greeted there by the Satan-like Zimoveikin, he is pressed against a fence "as though with tongs" in a courtyard where firewood is stored. The allusion here is to the fiery furnace of Perdition.

The people emerge from the houses, bars, taverns and the fleamarket (*tolkuchii rynok*, suggestive of shoving and grinding). Prokharchin's attention is especially attracted by a "sinful woman" (*greshnaia baba*) dressed in rags and bast sandals [251]. She brandishes her crutch and outshouts even the firemen as she rambles incoherently about how her children have turned her out and about two five-kopek coins which she has lost. Children and kopeks are hopelessly confused in her speech, much as money is linked with a fictitious filial relationship in Prokharchin's life. The "sinful woman" is an emanation of Prokharchin's fallen spirit. As she continues shouting, oblivious to the sparks and cinders that are flying all around, Prokharchin is suddenly overcome by terror as he realizes that "there is something behind all of this and he isn't going to get off scot-free." [251]

At this point, a man in tattered peasant dress and with singed hair and beard begins shouting in order to rally the crowd (*ves' Bozhii narod*: literally, 'God's entire nation') against Prokharchin. The miser freezes in terror when he recognizes the man as a cabdriver whom he deceived five years earlier, slipping away without paying the fare and "lifting his heels as he ran, as though he were running barefoot across a white-hot metal plate."[8] The enraged crowd entwines Prokharchin "like a many-colored dragon" (*podobno pestromu zmeiu*), crushing and strangling him. Dostoevsky's portrayal of the crowd in this hellish episode as both a dragon and a flowing stream brings to mind icon depictions of the Last Judgment, in which sinners descend into Hell along a serpent-like river of fire.[9]

Waking up, Prokharchin imagines that he is on fire together with his entire corner and, most important, his mattress. He clutches the mattress and flees from his partitioned corner, but the other lodgers find him and carry him back to his bed.

> ...they carried him triumphantly back behind the partitions, which, incidentally, were not on fire at all. All that was on fire was Semyon Ivanovich's head. There they laid him back in bed. In the same way the tattered, unshaven, stern organ grinder places his Pulcinella back in his travelling case after it has raised a ruckus, beat everyone up, and sold its soul to the Devil. Until a new presentation, it must end its existence in the same trunk with that very same Devil and with the negroes, Petrushka, Mademoiselle Katerina and with her lucky lover the overseer-captain. [251-52]

The trunk in this extended simile is a metaphor for the grave. "Seduced" by Zimoveikin, Prokharchin has sold his soul to the Devil. The "new presentation" for which he must wait is the Second Coming of Christ and the end of the world.[10] In Russian church lore, including icons of the Last Judgment, demons are portrayed as black men. Mademoiselle Katerina and her officer-lover correspond, respectively, to the landlady (Prokharchin's conscience, soul, or the good part of his spirit) and a symbolic Elijah the Prophet such as Iaroslav Il'ich. The Russian term for the "overseer captain" is *kapitan ispravnik*, derived from *ispravit'* ('to correct', 'to set straight') and suggestive once again of Elijah's function as an enforcer of divine retribution. Here the landlady's remark that "she knows even Iaroslav Il'ich and, had she wanted, she could have become an ober-officer's wife long ago" becomes doubly significant.[11] In this symbolic context, it seems likely that Dostoevsky associated Petrushka with St. Peter, who guards the gates to Heaven. Thus, all the puppets in this passage have spiritual analogues: Prokharchin's corrupted self, his soul, the Devil, demons, Elijah and St. Peter.

Finally, Prokharchin "stretches out his legs and sets out along the path of his sins and good deeds." [259] The final shock which precipitates his death is Zimoveikin's attempt to rob him at night. Added to the spectacle of the fire and the miser's fears that his employment and income will be terminated, this trauma is too much for him. Soon Iaroslav Il'ich arrives "with his following." The word *prichet* is used in the figurative meaning 'following,' but its primary meaning is 'church-goers,' or a 'church congregation.' It points to the symbolic, spiritual significance of the "fierce son of Elijah." Like Elijah, who oversees Judgment, Iaroslav Il'ich arrives to preside over the final phase of Prokharchin's symbolic retribution. His arrival is heralded by allusions to an executor (*ekzekutor* also means 'executioner') and to a housefire immediately following word-play with *grekh* ('sin'). These are further clues that the author indeed has Elijah the Prophet in mind:

> Mr. Prokharchin stretched out his legs and set out along the path of his good and bad deeds. It is uncertain whether Semyon Ivanovich was frightened by something... or whether there was some other reason [*grekh*], but the fact is that even if the executor himself had appeared in the apartment and personally given Semyon Ivanovich his dismissal [*Abschied*] for freethinking, reckless behavior and drunkenness... even if Semyon Ivanovich had immediately received a reward [cf. "retribution" in the housefire episode], or if, finally, the house had caught fire and Semyon Ivanovich's head had begun to burn, he might have not even deigned to stir a finger at the news. [259]

As Iaroslav Il'ich examines the scene of Prokharchin's

death, the miser's body is pushed off the bed so that his bony legs jut upward "like two branches on a tree that has been burned" [260]. Once again the allusion is to the fire of retribution and probably to the lightning of Elijah the Prophet. Iaroslav Il'ich exposes the "ignoble" contents of Prokharchin's trunk and raises a whirling storm (*buria*) of fluff from the mattress as he removes the miser's horde of 2497 rubles. Prokharchin's "ignoble" trunk, with its rags and junk, symbolizes his ignoble spirit. The trunk's contents simply "smell of a coffer" (*pakhlo zalavkom*), a pun based on the similar words *zalavkom* ('coffer') and *zolovkoi* ('sister-in-law'). Instead of a sister-in-law, Prokharchin's only claim to any nobility of soul, the lodgers find a coffer full of junk!

The concept of Prokharchin's guilt and of final Judgment lies at the heart of the story. It is hinted at with casual *double entendres* throughout the narrative. When Prokharchin is brought home after the fire, the term *vinovatyi* is applied to him. Here it is used in a secondary meaning, 'the victim,' or 'the person who is the cause of the commotion,' but its basic meaning is 'the guilty one.' The driver who brings him home suggests that Prokharchin might have had a stroke or a mild epileptic seizure, but the lodgers decide "there must be another cause."[12] The term *grekh* is used here colloquially in the meaning 'cause,' but its basic meaning is 'sin.' This usage of *grekh* is repeated in the passage about Prokharchin's death, cited above.

As noted above, Dostoevsky enriches his story with a chain of motifs derived from Pushkin's immortal masterpiece "The Queen of Spades." In both stories, the all-consuming passion of the central character is to grow rich. An important difference is that Pushkin's Germann has an altruistic goal of sorts – to improve the life of his descendants as well as his own – while Prokharchin has none. Germann hopes to learn a secret series of winning cards from an old countess who has inherited the secret from St. Germain. He obtains the secret, but causes the countess' death in the process. The cards are Three, Seven and Ace. Germann wins on the Three and the Seven, but he mistakenly plays a Queen of Spades instead of the Ace, losing the fortune he has amassed on the first two cards. He goes mad and is taken to an insane asylum.

When he first learns the secret, the winning cards become an obsession for him. A young girl reminds him of a Three of Hearts. Portly gentlemen remind him of the Ace. When asked the time of day, he replies: "Five to the Seven." When Germann looks into the coffin at the funeral of the old countess, she winks at him. Later, the Queen of Spades squints and laughs at him when he makes his fateful error at the gambling table.

On one plane of interpretation, Germann is simply a common man who attempts to rise above his fate and fails. But numerous details point to a second level of interpretation on which the countess is a symbol of tsarist authority, while Germann represents rebellious forces from below which would usurp that authority. He is compared to Napoleon and linked symbolically with the Russian Freemasons, whose secret meetings provided a forum for a relatively free expression of liberal ideas concerning government and society.[13] On this symbolic plane, Germann is a rebel and a freethinker who wants to rise above "Queen" and "King." He would become "Ace," the highest of cards which is at the same time a "One," a symbol here of the individual unfettered by royalty. Like Faust in his quest for life and happiness, Germann virtually sells his soul to the Devil, causing the countess' death and cruelly taking advantage of her young protégée. He is said to have "the profile of Napoleon and the soul of Mephistopheles."

It is with an eye to "The Queen of Spades" that Dostoevsky weaves the words "freethinker" (*vol'nodumets*) and "Napoleon" into the speech of Zimoveikin and a lodger as they attempt in vain to reason with the crazed miser. When Prokharchin rambles on about his fears that his office might be eliminated, Zimoveikin replies:

> "...You freethinker! I'll report you! What are you? Who are you? A rebel? You ram's head!..." [256]

The lodger Mark Ivanovich uses the same formulas in speaking ironically of Napoleon:

> "...What are you? You're a ram! You haven't a stake nor a house to your name! Do you think you're the only person there is in this world? Who are you? Napoleon? Are you Napoleon or not? Speak up, sir! Are you Napoleon or aren't you?" [257]

Of course, Prokharchin's "freethinking" is limited to his avarice; his "Napoleonic dream" is concealed inside his mattress. Even the thought of minor bureaucratic reform instills fear in the soul of this petty little "Napoleon." His miser's dream hinges on preservation of the status quo. Or, at least, so he thinks. For this reason it is fitting that he virtually becomes the Queen of Spades after he dies, winking lasciviously like the countess and the Queen which Germann plays by mistake:

> His little right eye was somehow rakishly squinting. It seemed that Semyon Ivanovich wanted to say something, to convey something extremely important, to explain himself without losing any time, as quickly as possible because there were urgent matters at hand... One could seem to hear him say [to the landlady]: "What's wrong with you? Do you hear, silly woman? Quit your bawling! Get some sleep, do you hear? I've died now, you see. No reason to cry now! Really! Lying here isn't so bad... But that's not what I

wanted to say. You're an Ace, woman, a real Ace! Do you understand? So now I've died. But then, well, if you don't mind my saying so, that can't be! So, well then, I haven't died. You hear? So what if I just get up, huh?" [263][14]

Prokharchin's calling his landlady an "Ace" (*tuz*) culminates an entire chain of card and number motifs which hearken back to the series of cards in "The Queen of Spades." The office worker Andrei Efimovich, who refers to his seven children as he counts his pay, was mentioned above. Curious turns of speech hint at an underlying connection between the seven children and a playing card of that number. One is the elliptical formulation "I have seven, sir" instead of the full form "seven children" when the children have not previously been mentioned. In Russian, this passage reads "*a u menia, sudar', semero-s*." Standing alone in this manner, *semero* is quite similar to the term for a Seven in a deck of cards: *semerka*. More striking is another phrase in which children are once again not mentioned directly:

> Semyon Ivanovich became exceedingly frightened, and although he was entirely certain of his own innocence concerning the unpleasant confluence of the number seven under one roof, it was as if it actually turned out that Semyon Ivanovich, and none other, was to blame. [250][15]

The number is linked on the "real" plane with children, following the pattern of Pushkin's story, where a little girl reminds Germann of the Three of Hearts. It is in Prokharchin's feverish delirium that Efimovich appears "as an apparition" (*kak prizrak*) and speaks of the number seven. The old countess appears to Germann as a ghost soon after her death and tells him the secret numbers. Besides the "sinful woman" who speaks confusedly of five-kopek coins (*piataki* 'fives') and her children, Prokharchin also dreams of a man with a four-ruble note in his hand. The term used is *chetverka*, the same word which refers to a Four in a deck of playing cards. He is rushing home, "where his wife, his little daughter and money amounting to thirty and a half (in the corner under the feather mattress) were all on fire." Thus, three apparitions appear in Prokharchin's apocalyptic dream with veiled allusions to the secret numbers of "The Queen of Spades." However, while Germann's Three-Seven-Ace symbolizes a measured upward progression toward power and freedom, the numbers in Prokharchin's dream represent only a maniac's hording of money in all denominations.

Like Germann, Prokharchin never gambles for fun with his comrades. Gambling, though, is a favorite pastime of the other lodgers. Significantly, they play cards when he lies in bed delirious after the fire.

Prokharchin repeatedly calls Zimoveikin an "Ace" (*tuz*). He also calls Zinovii Ivanovich a "Joker" (*shut*), but it is intimated that this term would be more appropriately applied to Zimoveikin.[16] In the stream of abuse which he unleashes against Zinovii Ivanovich, Prokharchin includes the words "you Joker-dog" (*pes shut*). A moment later, the Mephisthophelean Zimoveikin enters the room, "sniffing all about" like a dog. Moreover, "Joker" refers to the Devil in Russian expressions such as *Shut ego znaet* (The Joker only knows).

When Zimoveikin first met Prokharchin, the reader is told, he stole his new breeches. Dostoevsky takes care to employ the genitive case so that the word meaning 'breeches' (*reituzy*) ends in -*tuz*, sounding like the word for "Ace."

Another cryptic, playful allusion to cards and "The Queen of Spades" is the remark (cited above) that Prokharchin has "neither a stake nor a house to his name" (*ni kola ni dvora*). The basic meaning of Russian *kol* is 'a wooden stake,' although in the Russian idiom just cited it actually refers to a plot of land designated by stakes used as boundary markers; i.e. "a stake of land." But by virtue of a stake's resemblance to the numeral One, *kol* is sometimes used in reference to a "One."[17] *Dvor* refers to a farmhouse in the expression used here, but it can also refer to a royal court. Thus, the old idiom hints at a second meaning: Prokharchin has neither an Ace nor any royal cards in his hand. Like Germann's dream, Prokharchin's miserable "Napoleonic dream" is only a delusion: death is approaching.[18]

The message is much the same as that of Prokharchin's name, derived from *prokharchit'sia* ('to go broke spending all one's money on food'). Prokharchin skimps on food for twenty-five years in order to save his kopeks, but Elijah strips him of his tiny fortune when his time of Judgment comes.

Pushkin's treatment of Germann is characteristically detached; there is no moralising about Germann's recklessness in relation to the countess or his cruelty toward the young ward. Germann's attempt to obtain the secret card combination is presented symbolically as a struggle to rise above an abstract Fate. Pushkin's narrator does not place his tale in an explicitly ethical or religious framework. If any moral or religious lessons are to be drawn, the reader must interpolate them himself. In "Mr. Prokharchin," Dostoevsky harnesses Fate to Elijah's chariot. He combines Pushkin's classical, pagan theme of an impersonal Fate with the traditional Christian view of God as the ultimate Arbiter. For this reason, the thematic thrust of his story is different. Pushkin portrays primarily the struggle of the individual personality against authority in all its potential forms, including the Czar and – conceivably – God; Dostoevsky portrays the contest waged between man's fallen spirit and – specifically – God.

Part Four: *The Landlady* and *The Idiot*

> *"I can't stand prophets and epileptics, especially these emissaries of God."*
> – Ivan Karamazov

The early novella *The Landlady* is probably the least understood of all of Dostoevsky's works. Most critics find it so perplexing that they devote little attention to it or choose to ignore it altogether. Belinsky was frankly baffled by the tale. Soon after its first publication, he wrote:

> Not only the main theme of this seemingly interesting tale, but even its basic *sense* will remain an enigma to us until the author publishes the necessary explanations and interpretations for this wondrous riddle of his far-fetched imagination. What exactly is it? An abuse of talent or an impoverished talent which is striving to climb higher than its abilities permit and, therefore, fears to go the usual route and seeks a path that has never been heard of before? We do not know the answer, but it seems to us that the author wants to reconcile Marlinsky with Hoffman, mixing in a little new-fangled humor and smearing on some Russian folklore for frosting[...]. There is not a single simple, lifelike word or expression in this entire tale. Everything is contrived, stilted, artificial and false.[1]

Critics' understanding of *The Landlady* has advanced very little since Belinsky wrote this appraisal in 1847. The dearth of scholarship devoted to this story is testimony to the puzzlement which it engenders.[2]

However, a key to the "riddle" is once again the folkloric figure of Elijah the Prophet. As in the story "Mr.

Prokharchin," written before *The Landlady*, and works such as *Stepanchikovo*, which come later, a symbolic representative of divine wrath bearing the name *Il'ia* (Elijah) stands at the thematic center of the tale. Like Elijah "Gunpowder" in *Crime and Punishment*, he is repeatedly associated with thunder, lightning and fire. The blast of his rifle echoes the divine thunder, while the flash of his knife reflects the lightning of Elijah the Prophet.

As the story first opens, a young man – Vasilii Mikhailovich Ordynov – goes out in search of a room. He has lived a solitary existence for three years after completing his university studies and receiving a small inheritance – enough to live on for about three years. He has been writing a tract which deals with the history of the church and formulates his own original "system," a term which doubtless signifies a socialist or utopian theory.[3] The "wonderful, joyous image of his idea" is only beginning to emerge from his soul, and "the time for its incarnation and realization was still far off, possibly very far off, and maybe even altogether *impossible!*"[4] Living as a recluse, entirely cut off from the real world, Ordynov has "thoroughly grown wild" (*odichal sovershenno*). His own spiritual "wildness" seems to be mirrored by his landlady, an elderly widow who now moves away "to some backwoods" (*v glush'*), as though his own soul had left him. Her moving away forces him to look for another room.

Ordynov eperiences an unexpected joy and exhilaration as he wanders along the Petersburg streets. His pale cheeks grow ruddy and his eyes seem to flash with "new hope" as he breathes the cold, fresh air and observes the noisy, animated life around him. Isolated in his stuffy little room, he had forgotten about the real world outside:

> It hadn't entered his head that there was another life – noisy, thunderous, eternally troubled, eternally changing, eternally calling and, sooner or later,

unavoidable. [265]⁵

Thus, at the very outset it is suggested that Ordynov's emerging theory is divorced from reality and impossible to realize, while the life which he has turned away from is inescapable.

Ordynov listens in fascination to the speech of the people around him and seems to examine the conclusions he has drawn in the solitary silence of his room. But his head begins to reel from the "noise, lustre and whirlwind" of life, and he is overcome by sadness:

> A melancholy and sorrow took hold of him. He began to worry about his whole life, about everything he did and even about his future. A new thought was giving him no peace. It suddenly dawned on him that he had been alone all his life, that nobody had loved him and he hadn't been fortunate enough to love anyone else. [267]

Haunted by recollections of the solitariness of his entire life, Ordynov wanders into an outlying, deserted part of town and eats in a lonely tavern. His surroundings are gloomy, dark and unfriendly. But then he wanders into a church, which at first is illuminated through a narrow window in the cupola by the rays of the setting sun. As the sun sets, the holy lamps and candles take over, illuminating the gilded icons with their glowing flames.

Overcome by deep anguish and "a certain suppressed feeling," Ordynov leans against the wall in a dark corner and momentarily drifts into forgetfulness. He is aroused when an old man resembling a merchant enters the church, accompanied by a beautiful young woman. The old man is dressed in native Russian fashion. A "fiery gaze" (*ognevoi vzgliad*) flashes from beneath his gloomy, overhanging eyebrows. The young woman kneels before the icon of the Virgin and prays mournfully. Illuminated by the icon lamps, tears can be seen streaming down her face. When they leave the church, Ordynov follows the couple as far as the gateway of the building where they live, but when the old man turns and looks at him rather menacingly, he returns to his room. He lights a candle, and the image of the weeping woman, embodying rapture and adoration as well as horror and childlike contrition, rises before his imagination to torment him.

The next morning, Ordynov sets out *in the opposite direction* and rents a room from a German who lives alone with his daughter. Ordynov pays a deposit and the German, nicknamed Spiess (cf. *Spiessbürger*: 'philistine'), praises him for his love of science and learning. Promising to return with his belongings in the evening, Ordynov heads back to his room, but suddenly changes direction and returns to the church where he saw the mysterious couple. After a long wait, however, the couple fails to appear, and Ordynov leaves the church, his face flushed as he "stubbornly suppresses a certain feeling which urged itself upon him independently of his own will." In an effort to change his train of thought, he eats again at yesterday's tavern and wanders outside of town "into the backwoods" (*v glush'*). But the lonely scene which he encounters there only depresses him: "dead silence;" an emaciated horse; a broken wheel; a dog which growls as it gnaws its bone; and a baby, scratching its head and clothed only in a miserable shirt. The miserable scene seems to reflect the loneliness and sterility of the hermit's life which Ordynov has been living. He heads back toward "the city, out of which came the sonorous ringing of the bells as they summoned all to the evening service."

In the church, he now finds the mysterious couple and kneels down beside the young woman. Her face, illuminated once again by the church lamps, expresses "boundless piety" and her tears "seem to wash away some terrible crime." Overcome by a feeling that is both rapture and torment, Ordynov breaks into sobs and presses his feverish head to the cold church floor. This outpouring of his soul comes after all the tiring, sleepless nights of "stifling and endless silence amid unconscious longings and unbearable spiritual throes;" it is compared to a thunderstorm:

> [...] just as the whole sky suddenly grows black on a hot, humid day and a thunderstorm begins to pour rain and fire down onto the thirsting land, clinging to the emerald branches with pearls of rain, smashing down the grass and fields, beating down to the ground the flowers' little cups so that, afterwards, when the sun's first rays appear, everything will again come to life and rise toward the sun, triumphantly sending its sweet incense up to the heavens, rejoicing at its life renewed... [271]

As the young woman leaves the church, she becomes "all aflame like the glow of the sunset" (*budto zarevom*) when she turns to look back at Ordynov. A "strange enmity" grips the young man's heart when his eyes meet the "bilious and mocking gaze" of the old man as he walks away from the church.

The next morning, Ordynov seeks out the mysterious couple's apartment with the wild hope of renting a room from them. He must climb a muddy, dilapidated *spiral stairway* to reach their apartment on the top floor. Before ascending the stairs, he passes a Tatar janitor and a *coffinmaker* who lives on the ground floor. The old man, "as pale as death," greets him surlily at the door, but the young woman intercedes and willingly rents him a tiny room. Its most notable features are a gilt icon and icon lamp on a shelf in the corner and a large Russian stove. The old man asks for Ordynov's passport and introduces himself as *Il'ia Murin*, a merchant (*meshchanin*).

The spiral stairway in this story is a precursor of the spiral stairway leading to the police station in *Crime and*

Punishment. It is suggestive of a whirlwind ascent into a higher spiritual realm where Elijah the Prophet resides. In passing the coffinmaker, Ordynov symbolically climbs beyond the realm of mortality for a duel with Elijah.

Ordynov's head *spins* as he unpacks his belongings: *dobro*, used here with a tinge of irony. It might be rendered well with English 'goods': the symbolic implication is that the only good deeds which Ordynov can present to Elijah at Judgment are his books and anticlerical writings. Murin takes Ordynov's passport and tells him to "live with peace" (an apparent *double entendre* addressed to Ordynov, who has cut himself off from the real world: *zhivi s mirom* 'live with peace,' which might also be read literally as 'live with the world'). Although Ordynov had hoped for another glimpse at the beautiful woman, Murin immediately retreats inside, closing the door. Ordynov feels a hatred for Murin growing inside him:

> For some unknown reason it wasn't easy for him to even look at the old man. There was something contemptuous and spiteful in his eyes. But this unpleasant impression soon faded. For three days now Ordynov had been living in a sort of *whirlwind* in comparison with his former quiet life; but he was in no condition to sort it all out in his mind. In fact, he was afraid to. Everything in his life had gone topsy-turvy; he vaguely felt that his life had been broken in two. A single urge, a single expectation had taken control of him and no other thought concerned him. [273]

After an old servant woman gives Ordynov dinner, he tries to read, but finding that he cannot concentrate, he decides to go for a walk:

> Walking at random, not even seeing the road, he tried as best he could to concentrate (*sosredo-*

tochit'sia dukhom), to gather his fragmentary thoughts and to think over his situation somewhat. But the effort only flung him into *suffering and torment*. Chills and fever seized him by turns, and at times his heart suddenly began to pound so hard that he had to lean against a wall for support. "No, death is better," he thought. "Death is better," he whispered through feverish, trembling lips, giving little thought to what he was saying. He walked for a long time. Finally, noticing that he was drenched to the bone and that the *rain was pouring down* in bucketfuls, he returned home. [274]

As in *Crime and Punishment*, Elijah the Prophet brings pressure to bear on a transgressor with his rainstorm. For Ordynov a symbolic time of Judgment has arrived.

When it grows dark, Ordynov goes to Murin's room in order to "obtain fire" (*dostat' ognia*), but the door is locked. The old servant woman gives him some matches. He soon drifts off to sleep and dreams that he rises from bed and stumbles, falling onto a stack of firewood, when Murin returns from vespers. This motif is a variation on the stack of firewood in "Mr. Prokharchin" and the allusion to Raskolnikov's being burned to death in the first scene at the police station in *Crime and Punishment*. Here once again, the symbolic allusion is to the fires of Hell and Judgment. Ordynov attempts, like Prometheus, to usurp the fire of the divine thunderer, but then finds himself threatened by the flames of Judgment.

He wakes up to find the young woman, Katerina, looking after him in his illness. She is an incarnation of the purest, most unselfish love, while Ordynov, starved for love by a life that has known only loneliness, yearns for her passionately. She represents the divine aspect of Ordynov's spirit; she is his soul. Her symbolic role closely resembles that of Zarnitsyna, Raskol'nikov's landlady. Both are landladies, or spiritual *mistresses* on the symbolic plane. Both are associated with celestial light: Katerina with the sunset (*zaria*) and its glow (*zarevo*), Zarnitsyna with the glow of lightning (*zarnitsa*).[6] They are meek figures who, at least in the imagination of the central hero, are tortured by a symbolic Elijah. Katerina's tearful, mournful aspect links her with the "lady in mourning" in *Crime and Punishment* and with Trusotsky, who wears the symbol of mourning in *The Eternal Husband*. Symbolically, she mourns for Ordynov's fallen spirit.

Katerina's symbolic spiritual role is highlighted by an intricate network of imagery and deceptively casual expressions with manifold meanings. To the feverish Ordynov the room seems to be spinning as Katerina talks to him. She tells him that when he gets well, they will live "as brother and sister." When Ordynov asks where she is from, she only replies, "I'm not from these parts." She talks of love and notes that "books, they say, ruin a person." Then she asks whether Ordynov likes to pray. Clearly, Katerina enters the story as an antithesis to Ordynov's intellectual, anticlerical activity.

When Murin arrives and Katerina goes to join him, Ordynov in his delirium experiences glimpses of hellish doom and heavenly rapture:

> [...] the thought flitted through his mind that he was condemned to live in a long, unending sleep filled with strange, fruitless alarms, struggle and suffering. In horror he tried to rise up against the ominous fatalism that was stalking him, but in a moment of strained, desperate struggle an unknown power would vanquish him once again, and he could clearly feel how he would lose his memory and how an impassable, bottomless darkness would open before him, and he would fly headlong into it with a cry of anguish and desperation. But at times there were moments of unbearable, even

> destructive happiness, when life's essence frenziedly intensifies throughout one's whole being, when the past becomes perfectly clear, when the present bright moment rings with triumph and joy, and one dreams clearly of the unknown future; [...] and one hails a life resurrected and renewed. [277-78]

He perceives his fever as hellish flames which torment him and consume his blood. But then he feels (or imagines) Katerina's burning tears falling onto his face and a long, gentle kiss which opens before him a vision of his childhood.

First he sees a blissful picture of infancy and early childhood, when bright spirits hovered around his cradle and he knew only happiness and his mother's love. But suddenly a "mean old man" begins to appear before him, peering from behind every bush and from beneath every letter of his grammar book, laughing, grimacing and teasing him. The boy vaguely senses that his entire future is in the hands of the gnome-like old man, who brings "the slow poison of grief and tears" into his life, instilling in him an "unchildlike horror." The old man takes away from the boy his mother and begins to whisper to him a long, wondrous fairytale that is "incomprehensible to the heart of a child." It tortures the boy and fills him with horror and "an unchildlike passion." He becomes aware that he is alone in a hostile world and wonders why he is here, suspecting that he has wandered into a den of bandits (*zlodeiskii priton*). At night, an old woman begins to whisper the same long fairytale, but now the fairytale assumes striking forms which rise before the boy's imagination. He sees luxurious, enchanted gardens; cities rising and falling; cemeteries sending out to him their dead; and finally:

> He felt himself die, becoming only dust, without

resurrection, forever and ever. He wanted to flee, but there was no corner in the whole universe where he might seek refuge. [280]

The long fairytale which instills horror in the boy is the story of real life, of the real world of sin and corruption. It is the story of man's fall and exile from the "luxurious, enchanted garden" and of the apocalyptic doom and eternal death which await evildoers. The "mean old man" is an emanation of Elijah, the divine tormentor who rains down suffering on fallen man, forever reminding him of his fallen state.

When Katerina relates how Il'ia Murin took her away from her parents, Ordynov clearly sees in him the "mean old man" of his dream. He hears a "spiritual storm" in her words. "Her life becomes his life; her sorrow – his." Indeed, the story of Katerina's separation from her parents is the story of Ordynov's own spiritual coming of age, of the dawning of his own conscience. Katerina's tale (most likely a figment of Ordynov's delirious imagination) is a spiritual allegory which runs parallel to his dream about the "mean old man." It combines Biblical metaphors with the motifs of folklore and wedding ritual.

Katerina first tells about the stormy night when Murin came to buy her soul. The storm is so strong that it snaps an old oak tree outside Katerina's home and wrecks her father's boats on the river. At midnight, as she sits at home preparing a shroud for her dying mother, Murin comes knocking at their gates. He has always instilled fear in her and has never treated her gently. He enters their home, all wet from the storm, which has "driven him twenty versts." Neither Katerina nor her mother know where he resides. He flings down his hat and gloves and sits down "without praying to the icons, without bowing to the hosts" (*obrazam ne molitsia, khoziaevam ne klaniaetsia* – a variation on a formula pertaining to Il'ia Muromets in the *bylina* "Il'ia and the Huge Idol").[7] Speaking in Tatar with Katerina's mother, Murin "buys" the girl's soul and gives her a box of pearls. After he leaves, Katerina and her mother use the language of Russian wedding ritual in referring to Murin as a "merchant": *kuptsy byli, tovar pozabyli*... 'Merchants were here; they forgot their wares.' – a typical formula of the folk matchmaking ritual, referring to the party of the groom, who come to virtually buy the bride.[8] This groom, however, is the heavenly "groom" who comes at midnight.

Katerina returns to her room and listens to the storm all through the night. Five nights later, there is another storm when the "groom" returns to take away his bride; Katerina feels as though she is on fire and longs to go "to the edge of the world, *where the storm and lightning are born*." Appropriately, the symbolic Elijah returns at this moment. He kills Katerina's mother and causes her father's death by setting fire to his factory and evidently pushing him into a hot cauldron (*kotel*: also a term for a furnace, or boiler). Then, singed and smoking, Murin flees with Katerina to a "wide, wide river." When they climb into his boat and row away, "the shores disappeared in a glimmering." Murin then addresses this sea-like river:

> "Greetings, little mother, stormy little river! You give drink to God's people and me you feed! Have you watched my goods while I was gone? Are my wares intact? [...] For all I care you can take them all, stormy and insatiable as you are! Just so you promise to watch and cherish my one most valuable pearl! Spill at least a little word, fair maiden, shine in the storm like the sun, drive away the dark night with your light!" [298]

Murin is the "merchant" of Matthew 13:45-46, the same metaphor which later left an imprint on the final pages of *The Possessed*:

> 45 And the Kingdom of Heaven is like a merchant who seeks good pearls,
> 46 Who, finding one valuable pearl, went and sold all he had, and bought it.

It is a human soul which Murin "buys," sundering the parental bonds and setting its conscience free. As merchant of souls, he stores his wares in a "wide, wide," "stormy" river which seems vast and endless. The river is a symbol for the heaven above, refuge for redeemed souls and Katerina's longed-for source of storm and lightning.

After Katerina spends a year with Murin on the far side of the river, the young man Alyosha crosses the river to claim her as his betrothed. His words hint at the connection between Katerina's role as landlady (*khoziaika* 'mistress') and her symbolic function as an emanation of Ordynov's soul. He reproaches her for joining the "destroyer of souls" (literal rendering of *dushegubets* 'murderer') and taunts her for selling her soul:

> "[...] Buy my soul, too. Take it, mock my heart and my love, fair maiden. *Now I'm an orphan, my own master [khoziain], and my soul is my own, no one else's.* I've never sold it to anyone, unlike someone else who doused out her memory. But a heart isn't something to be bought. I'll give it to you for free; or is it, as it seems, a question of gain?" [300]

With the breaking of parental ties, Alyosha becomes the "master" of his soul; he is free to follow his own conscience. Ordynov, too, is without parents, and each attempts to wrest Katerina from Murin's domain. Alyosha lives entirely alone as he waits to carry Katerina away, while Ordynov lives as a recluse before his confrontation with Murin. Alyosha is a dream manifestation of Ordynov himself. Alyosha fails to win Katerina from Murin, who evidently pushes him into the river during a storm. This happens soon after Alyosha taunts Murin by suggesting that it might be his time to "drink the water;" i.e., to drink the bitter cup, to die. Similarly, Ordynov takes Murin's antique knife (an attempt to usurp Elijah's lightning) and approaches the old man as he lies in bed, intending to stab him. However, the attempt fails when Murin opens one eye and breaks into demonic laughter (a motif that was inspired by Pushkin's "Queen of Spades"), whereupon Ordynov trembles and drops the knife. Katerina then screams hysterically, "Alyosha! Alyosha!" Ordynov and Alyosha are further linked by the fact that this episode comes just after Ordynov and Murin drink wine, associated here with the "bitter cup" of suffering. Thus, Alyosha's claim to be "*master* of his own soul" elucidates the allegory of Ordynov's duel with Murin: consumed by his bookish plan for a rational world, Ordynov longs to free his spirit, or conscience, from all bonds with God in order to be the sole master of his actions, to be free of guilt and to answer to no divine *master* (*khoziain*: the landlord, Il'ia Murin, Elijah the Prophet) or spiritual *mistress* (*khoziaika*: the landlady, Katerina, Ordynov's divine aspect, his conscience). But Katerina, representing his conscience, chooses of her own free will to remain wed to Elijah. Ultimately, this implies that Ordynov's own conscience rejects his utopian system, which has evolved as a protest against the divine order with all the guilt, suffering and apparent injustice which it entails.

When Ordynov wakes up from his dream about the "mean old man," he peers through a crack in his wall and sees Murin and Katerina. Then, following an unconscious urge which "flares up in his blood like a housefire," he staggers to their door and forces his way into their room [281]. Murin's eyes "flash with enmity" and his face is distorted by wrath. He gropes for a rifle hanging on the wall and fires at Ordynov. The barrel "flashes" and the shot rings out, but he misses. When the smoke clears,

Ordynov sees Murin writhing in an epileptic seizure: *the falling sickness*. Like Smerdiakov's epileptic seizure in *The Brothers Karamazov* and Myshkin's seizure on the twisting stairway of The Scales Hotel when Rogozhin is about to stab him, Murin's attack (*pripadok*: from *padat'* 'to fall') of the falling sickness (*paduchaia bolezn'*) is intended to elicit associations with man's fall into sin. It is the "falling sickness" of Elijah the Prophet; i.e., the wrath which errant man incites in the fiery Avenger. Murin confesses that he almost stabbed Katerina with his knife during another seizure, and Ordynov's breaking into his room he attributes to the same "black weakness."

Thus, Ordynov encroaches on Murin's domain in a direct way three times: when he tries to enter Murin's room to "obtain fire;" when he breaks in and Murin fires his rifle; and when he threatens the old man with a knife. The fire and the knife on the wall are symbolic of Elijah's lightning; the flashing rifle, which also hangs on the wall, can be said to represent both the thunder and the lightning of the Prophet. Murin is also threatened by Alyosha as they row across the river, but in the end it is Alyosha himself who drinks the "bitter cup." His doom is foreshadowed by Murin when they meet beside the river: "Greetings, Alyosha, God help you! Have you lingered too long on the pier? Hurrying to your boats? [*na suda svoi pospeshaesh'?* 301]" The word *suda* ('boats') was carefully chosen for its associations with *sud* ('Judgment'). As it turns out, Alyosha is indeed hurrying to his Judgment and doom. And, according to a police official, Alyosha's demise evidently comes during another attack of Murin's "falling sickness."

Appropriately, the symbolic "Prophet" foretells the future for people who come to him to learn their fortunes. According to rumor, he correctly foretold the death of a young officer, and people whose fortunes he tells often go away as pale as death. When Ordynov asks the Tatar janitor about Murin's fortune-telling, he uses the verb *koldovat'*, which can refer to all kinds of black magic and wizardry. At the end of the tale, after his attempts to wrest Katerina from Murin have ended in failure, Ordynov compares himself with "that wizard's (*kolduna*) boastful apprentice who stole the magic word of his teacher and ordered the broom to fetch some water, but drowned when he forgot how to say 'Stop.'" Much as the wizard's apprentice fails to cope with the craft he has stolen, Ordynov fails to usurp the lightning of Elijah.

The central theme of *The Landlady* is that man carries within him a divine spark which will cause him to choose God's imperfect world of suffering, sin, guilt and atonement even though he has the freedom to prefer another arrangement. This is the same theme which lies at the heart of many of Dostoevsky's later works, including *Crime and Punishment*, where the murder of the old pawnbroker is the fruit of a scheme that is closely akin to Ordynov's utopian "system." Katerina – the symbol of Ordynov's own soul – is given the freedom to leave "Elijah" Murin at any moment, yet she freely chooses to remain with him. In parallel fashion, Ordynov finally abandons his "system" and turns to the Church:

> Now he reread that plan, reworked it, thought about it, read, labored over it, and finally rejected his idea, raising nothing on its ruins. But something resembling mysticism, predetermination and secret mystery began to penetrate his soul. The unfortunate fellow became aware of his sufferings and would ask God for healing. His German landlord's servant, a God-fearing old Russian woman, took great pleasure in telling how her quiet, humble roomer would pray, and how he would kneel motionless for hours at a time, with his forehead on the church floor... [318]

Katerina hints at the importance of the theme of free will

when she recites a proverb: "Freedom is sweeter than bread and more beautiful than the sun."[9] Of his own free will, Ordynov surrenders his freedom to God, just as Murin predicts:

> "[...] A weak man can't bear it alone. Just give him everything, and he'll return by himself and give everything back. Make him emperor of half the whole world [*poltsarstva zemnogo*], just try, and what do you think he'll do? He'll hide in a slipper, he'll turn so small. Give a weak man freedom, and he'll bind it up into a bundle and bring it back himself." [317]

The soul turns back to God like a flower turns to the sun. In his divine aspect, or soul, man senses the mysterious necessity and justice of his sufferings. Hence, the seemingly masochistic pleasure which Katerina derives from her sorrows:

> "[...] What is bitter to me and tears my heart is that I am his disgraced slave and the shame and disgrace are pleasing to me myself, shameless as I am, and it's pleasing for my heart to recall its sorrow, as though it were joy and happiness. My sorrow is that there is no strength in my heart and no anger for my wounds!.." [299]

After Katerina tells Ordynov the story of her "elopement" with Murin, she prepares to leave, saying: "Until tomorrow, my tears!" The tears stream down her face like dewdrops as she presses Ordynov's head to her breast and kisses him good-night. When he wakes up the next morning, his eyes are wet with tears and, like his own soul-symbol Katerina, he finds a strange pleasure in his suffering:

> He felt that the tears had not yet dried on his eyes – or had fresh, new tears splashed like a mountain spring from his flaming soul? And wonder of wonders! His torments were even sweet to him, although he vaguely felt with all his being that he could endure such punishment no longer. [302]

At the end of the story, it becomes apparent that Murin – Dostoevsky's symbolic Elijah the Prophet – in all likelihood is merely an ordinary criminal, like Koshmarov ('Mr. Nightmare'), the landlord who repeatedly pays him visits. Ordynov has, indeed, wandered into a den of thieves, as he feared in the dream about the "mean old man" of his childhood. This mirroring of God in a common thief reminds the reader of the coexistence of divine goodness and diabolic evil in man's nature, a major theme throughout the works of Dostoevsky. But the unexpected ending also serves to highlight the fact that Murin and Katerina, in their symbolic, spiritual roles, are primarily a reflection of the *inner* workings of Ordynov's soul, of his own *free will*. Indeed, much of his interaction with the mysterious couple he imagines in his delirium. His spiritual transformation comes not as the result of coercion or external forces; it is his own soul, guided by a divinely inspired conscience, which gravitates back toward God.

Murin's last name is that of St. Moisei Murin, a seventeenth-century Volga River pirate who sought atonement for his transgressions by living as a hermit in the wilderness.[10] An icon portrays him alongside Elijah the Prophet.[11] As a symbolic Elijah, Murin is a precursor of figures such as Il'ia Petrovich in *Crime and Punishment*. Like Il'ia Petrovich, he has both a "thunderous gaze" and a "gaze like lightning." His rifle brings to mind Il'ia Petrovich's nickname, "Gunpowder." His drinking wine with Ordynov – in a scene threaded with allusions to sorrow and bitterness – symbolically parallels the bitter cup of yellowish water that is held out to Raskol'nikov when he visits Il'ia Petrovich. Near the end of the story, at the police station, Murin diagnoses Ordynov's illness as the sad result of "too much book learning," while Il'ia Petrovich speaks disparagingly of writers, literati and students such as Raskolnikov. Imagery pertaining to fire is used again and again in the portrayal of Murin, as in that of Il'ia Petrovich. His eyes are continually "inflamed"; they "flash" (like lightning) and glow like hot coals, and he wears a fiery red scarf around his neck. Immediately after relating to Ordynov how she prays before the icon of the Virgin (referring to Her as *vladychitsa* 'The Mistress'), Katerina exclaims of Murin: "He is mighty! Great is his word!" [*On vlasten! Veliko ego slovo!* 294] The obvious Biblical style of these lines hints rather blatantly at Murin's divine significance.

Alongside Il'ia Murin, who is prominent in both dream and reality, there is another symbolic emanation of Elijah in the story: the policeman Iaroslav Il'ich (the same "fierce son of Elijah" who appears in "Mr. Prokharchin"). While Murin turns out to be a criminal, Iaroslav Il'ich has apparently been dismissed from his post by the final scene of the story, possibly because of infractions pertaining to Koshmarov's den of thieves. On the plane of everyday reality, both of these "Elijahs" turn out to be sinful souls. Both are part of the imperfect world which Ordynov comes to accept in the end.

Besides his name, Iaroslav Il'ich shares other attributes with the Russian folkloric Elijah and with his fictional descendant Il'ia Petrovich "Gunpowder." As a policeman, he is an enforcer of the law. He is "red-cheeked," lively and boisterous. Ordynov feels the ground shake beneath his feet (like the earthquake accompanying Elijah's ascent) just before he encounters Iaroslav Il'ich. (The ground also shakes as Il'ia Murin arrives in one scene.) Iaroslav Il'ich smokes a pipe "with a certain inspiration," while Raskolnikov complains about

"Gunpowder's" smoking a cigarette. He thanks Ordynov for "always bringing a balm (*bal'zam*)" [i.e., for his encouraging praise], a motif which can be related to the storm metaphor near the beginning of the story, in which the fields and flowers are said to send incense to the heavens after the storm. A chair "thunders" when Iaroslav Il'ich slides it across the floor, and he rides a "dashing buggy" (*likhie proletki*: derived from *letat'* 'to fly') which "comes flying," drawn by a pair of dashing *red horses*. His buggy is a creative variation on the icon portrayal of Elijah's chariot with its fiery red horses, and it is a literary antecedent for the buggy in which the police and fire chief Il'ia Il'ich "flies" about town in *The Possessed*.

Dostoevsky's characteristically double-edged portrayal of Iaroslav Il'ich hints repeatedly at his symbolic connection with Elijah the Prophet:

> Iaroslav Il'ich had the unusual tendency *to seek out good, noble people everywhere*, especially educated people who, at least by virtue of their talent and elegant behavior, are *worthy of belonging to higher society.* [...] In the tone of his voice there was *something bright, powerful and commanding which tolerated no dallying* [...] [283]

At the end of the story, Ordynov encounters Iaroslav Il'ich during a rainstorm. Soaked and muddy, and with a raindrop clinging "in some fantastic way" to the tip of his nose, he informs Ordynov that Koshmarov has been found to be the leader of a band of thieves, exclaiming:

> "After this, just try to judge about all of mankind! He was the head of the whole band! Their ringleader! Isn't that something?!"
>
> Iaroslav Il'ich spoke with feeling and, because of one man, he *passed judgment on all of mankind. Iaroslav Il'ich cannot do otherwise; it is in his*

character. [320]

"I always like to reward justice," he says to Ordynov. When Ordynov objects that he is too magnanimous, their dialog takes this peculiar turn:

> "No, I'm being perfectly just," Iaroslav Il'ich objected especially heatedly. *"What am I in comparison with you?* Well, isnt it the truth?"
> "Oh, *my God*!"
> *"Yes, sir..."*
> *Here a silence ensued.* [284]

Here Dostoevsky uses the same rather comical technique of *double entendre* that he later brings into play in *Stepanchikovo*, where the peasants address Egor Il'ich as their "lord" and "father."

After mentioning Pushkin's "amazing way of depicting human passion," Iaroslav Il'ich recommends his district doctor to the ailing Ordynov. In praising his expertise, he relates how the doctor "nobly" amputated the injured hand of a worker whose life was threatened by "Anthony's fire" (gangrene). The allusion is to the hellfire which threatens Ordynov's soul if his spiritual ailment (stemming from his "passion" for learning) is not healed. Later, Murin claims to know of a remedy for Ordynov's ailment, attributing his sickness to the books which have caused "mind and wisdom to get mixed up" (*um za razum zashel*).

Murin and Katerina are counterposed by Ordynov's German landlord and his daughter Tinchen. The two couples are symbolic antipodes. Unlike Murin, the German approves of Ordynov's interest in science and is even eager to join him in his studies. Murin sees a spiritual cure (implied on the symbolic plane) for Ordynov's sickness, while Tinchen sets about treating Ordynov when he rejoins them near the end of the story. She doubtless uses the conventional methods of western medicine and, judging by the fact that Ordynov remains ill for three more months, her treatment seems to leave much to be desired. The German is scrupulously precise in assessing Ordynov's rent, counting every kopek, while Murin even refuses to accept compensation for the time Ordynov has lived in his apartment. Iaroslav Il'ich extolls this "holy hospitality which rests with the Russian people." The opposition between Murin and the German is that between western rationalism and Russian spirituality. Details such as Murin's Russian garb and the Russian stove in his apartment serve to emphasize the symbolic importance of nationality in this work.[12] The many formulas and motifs from Russian folk songs and tales used in the portrayal of Murin and Katerina give the allegory of Ordynov's soul a specifically Russian coloring. And, of course, this can also be said of the Elijah symbolism, which is based on a specifically Russian folkloric perception of the Prophet.

Dostoevsky endows Murin with the intensely wrathful qualities of Elijah at the risk of misleading the reader. The fire of the Prophet and the Devil's hellfire are functionally similar and easy to confuse. Most readers and critics, unaware of the connections with Elijah, have tended to interpret Murin as a demonic figure.[13] Dostoevsky sets up signposts to guide the reader past this pitfall. Most notable is the scene in which Murin bluntly tells Katerina that he is not the Devil and proves it by crossing himself. However, in the final analysis, it is clear that "signposts" of this type have failed in their purpose. Ingenious as it is, *The Landlady* requires more attention to detail than readers are generally willing to give. Its many hints, word-plays and spiritual symbols are skimmed over by eyes that are in a hurry to reach the end of the story so that they can move on to works written in a more comfortable, realistic style.

A number of the central symbolic motifs of *The Landlady* foreshadow similar motifs in *The Idiot*. Each work becomes easier to understand when it is compared with the other. Katerina, a symbol of Ordynov's soul, is repeatedly associated with celestial light (the dawn, the sun etc.), as previously noted. When Ordynov first sees her, she is bathed in the light of the holy lamps which illuminate the church after the light of the setting sun ceases to penetrate the cupola. In this passage there is an implied association between Katerina and both the sunlight and the lamps. In *The Idiot*, Myshkin relates the story of a man who contemplates the sunlight as he is about to face a firing squad:

> In the near distance there was a church, and its gilt roof gleamed in the bright sun. He recalled that he stared fixedly at this roof and at the gleaming rays which it reflected; he couldn't tear himself away from those rays: it seemed to him that those rays were his new nature, and in three minutes he would somehow flow together with them. [I, 5]

Here, as in *The Landlady*, celestial light is associated with man's soul, his divine aspect. Myshkin also describes the moment immediately preceding his epileptic seizures as flashes of lightning which illuminate his entire being and magnify his spritual awareness:

> One of the things he was contemplating was a stage in his epilepsy which would come almost at the very onset of an attack (if the attack happened while he was awake) when suddenly amid depression, sadness and spiritual darkness there were moments when his brain seemed to flame up and all his lifestrength would intensify inside him with an uncommon force. His self-awareness and consciousness of life were magnified nearly tenfold at these moments, which continued like *lightning*. His mind and heart were illuminated (*ozarialos'*) by an unusual light; it was as though all his troubles, all his doubts, all his worries were reconciled at

once, resolved into a higher calm filled with a clear, harmonic joy and hope, filled with wisdom and a higher purpose. But these moments – these flashes – were still only a premonition of that final second (never more than a second) when the seizure itself began. Of course, this second was unbearable. When he thought about this moment after recovering from the attack, he often told himself: all of this *lightning* and these flashes of a higher consciousness and awareness - and, therefore, of a "higher realm" – are only an illness, an interruption of the normal condition; if this is true, then it can hardly be called a "higher realm", but one of the lowest instead. [...] "Well, and what if it is a sickness?" he finally decided. "What does it matter if it's an abnormal sort of tension if its result – the experience when it's recalled and contemplated afterwards in a healthy state – still proves to be harmony and beauty in the highest degree and gives you an unimaginable feeling of fulfillment, measure, reconciliation and rapturous prayerful coalescence with the highest synthesis of life?" [...] He could hardly doubt that it really was "beauty and prayer," that it really was "a higher synthesis of life," and he admitted no doubts. [II, 5]

Myshkin's thoughts of these *lightning* realizations come just after he passes a *knife shop* where Rogozhin, who is stalking him, has bought a knife. He then goes to visit Nastas'ia Filippovna, but does not find her at home. His conscience torments him because he feels he has betrayed his friend and "brother" Rogozhin by going to Nastas'ia. Meanwhile, as he returns to his hotel, named "The Scales," thunder can be heard in the distance and the air becomes stiflingly humid (*dushno*; cf. *dusha* 'soul'). Just as Myshkin enters the hotel gates, a thundercloud "swallows the evening light," "opens wide" and pours its storm down onto the city. He glimpses Rogozhin near the hotel, standing as his "judge and accuser," but represses all thoughts of either Rogozhin's or his own transgressions. When he climbs the hotel stairs, which wind around a central stone pillar (*stolb*; cf. *stolby* 'northern lightning display'), he sees Rogozhin hiding in a niche in the pillar. As Rogozhin raises the knife to stab him, Myshkin is seized by a violent attack of *the falling sickness*:

> Then suddenly something seemed to open wide before him: an uncommon *internal* light illuminated (*ozaril*) his soul. This moment lasted perhaps half a second; but he nevertheless clearly remembered the beginning, that very first sound of his own horrendous cry which came tearing from his lungs by itself and which he was powerless to stop. Then he immediately lost consciousness, and complete darkness set in. [II, 5]

Myshkin falls in convulsions to the bottom of the stairs. Those who find him there speculate about the accident:

> Had the man simply fallen or "had there been some sin" (*byl kakoi grekh*)? Soon, however, they recognized the falling sickness.

The careful juxtaposition of *sin* and *falling sickness* underscores the symbolic associations of Myshkin's fall. In Rogozhin, as in the criminal Il'ia Murin, the wrath of Elijah the Prophet is reflected. His knife, like Murin's knife, is the lightning of the divine Judge and Accuser. Myshkin, a mortal sinner, ascends the spiral staircase (the whirlwind of Elijah) to face Judgment. Hence, the name of the hotel, "The Scales," inspired by the Apocalypse and icons of the Last Judgment in which men's sins and virtues are weighed on a set of hanging scales. Hence, too, Myshkin's citation from the Apocalypse in his description of the epileptic seizures:

> [...] at this moment I somehow come to understand the strange saying that *time will be no more*. [II, 5]

After ascending on the "whirlwind," Myshkin faces a figure of retribution associated with Elijah and the eternal Judgment of his own conscience. "Elijah" gives him a glimpse of the divine light of Truth before he tumbles back down into his normal, fallen state. But these brief glimpses of Heaven, like illuminations of conscience, serve as a guiding inspiration in Myshkin's life.

Part Five: *The Eternal Husband*

> *The weather was bad that morning in Mokroye. Clouds darkened the whole sky and the rain came down by the bucketful.*
> — *The Brothers Karamazov*

Dostoevsky wrote his short novel *The Eternal Husband* in Dresden in the fall and winter of 1869, after completing *The Idiot* and before beginning work on *The Possessed*. It was published in Strakhov's journal *The Dawn* in the first two issues of 1870. Strakhov himself considered *The Eternal Husband* one of the "deepest and most interesting" of Dostoevsky's works, although he was doubtless prejudiced by the fact that he was the publisher.[1] At any rate, he predicted that most readers would not really understand the work and, judging by published reviews of the novel and by recent Soviet literary studies, his prediction was correct. V.P. Burenin, for example, denigrated the "morbid false psychology" and "nervous dialogs" of the novel, paying no heed to the spiritual allegory and symbolic technique which lie at its very heart.[2] A reviewer in *The Voice* wrote enthusiastically about "a certain mystery, some sort of secret which lurks in all the seemingly banal aspects of life" portrayed in the novel, but there is nothing to suggest that the reviewer had fathomed the mystery himself.[3]

Before beginning to write *The Eternal Husband*, Dostoevsky used the words "my usual theme" (*moia vsegdashniaia sushchnost'*) in characterizing the work as he envisioned it.[4] He compared it to *Notes from the Underground*, but a comparison with *Crime and Punishment* would have been even more apt, judging by the finished product. The symbolic network which generates the central theme of the novel can best be understood in light of parallel symbols in *Crime and*

Punishment.
Like *Crime and Punishment*, *The Eternal Husband* is the story of a sinner's path to confession. Unlike Raskol'nikov, however, he does not confess in the end. The central character, Vel'chaninov, is an outgoing, cynical man of the world who has lived a profligate's life, squandering fortunes and flitting from lover to lover. Filled with "arrogant self-confidence," his eyes no longer shine with "clarity and goodness" and his complexion has lost its former "feminine softness." [6][5] He has fallen from innocence into corruption.

As the narrative opens, Vel'chaninov is tormented by a certain anxiety (*toska*). He suffers from memories of "crimes" he has committed and debts he never paid. The narrator is careful to point out that Vel'chaninov's malady goes deeper than the "verdicts of his mind alone." It seems to Vel'chaninov that the recollections of his crimes are being presented to him from a new, unfamiliar point of view by someone else, an external force. He tries to joke to himself:

> "[...] Somebody out there is concerned for my morality and is sending me these damned memories and tears of repentance." [9]

He consults a doctor about his new anxiety, which tends to come at night. The doctor comments on the phenomenon of divided personality and recommends a change in lifestyle and possibly a laxative as well, a motif which seems to mock the very notion that the problem is a physical ailment or simply a problem of clinical psychology.

Meanwhile, July approaches with all the heat, dust and stiflingness (*dukhota*) typical of Petersburg. Vel'chaninov had planned to leave Petersburg by July, but decided to stay after his lawsuit took a bad turn in March, the same time his attacks of anxiety began. But he derives a certain "pleasure" from the stifling city with "the mouse-like hurry-scurry of its civil servants" and "the cowardliness of their miserable souls" (*truslivost' ikh dushonok*). Every day he subjects himself to a cheap, unpalatable dinner at a cafe on Nevsky, by the *Police Bridge*. It seems to him that there is "something morbid" in this self-imposed ordeal.

It is at this cafe that he comes to a sudden realization one stifling day, the third of July. He sits down at his table "in nasty spirits" (*v samom skverneishem raspolozhenii dukha*), casts his hat aside "with all his heart" (*s serdtsem*), and sinks into thought. Then it dawns on him that what has been bothering him recently is a man in mourning whom he has encountered on the street on five different occasions. The man wears a hat with a ribbon of black crepe to symbolize mourning. He seems somehow familiar to Vel'chaninov, like an old acquaintance who has been long forgotten, but Vel'chaninov cannot recollect who he might be. That night he dreams that a crowd has gathered in his doorway, accusing him of a crime. They all wait for a silent man sitting at a table – clearly the man in mourning – to pass judgment on Vel'chaninov. Enraged, Vel'chaninov begins to beat the man, hitting him again and again until the bell at the door rings loudly three times. Then he wakes. Shortly thereafter, at three in the morning, the man with the crepe on his hat pays him a visit. He turns out to be Pavel Pavlovich Trusotskii, whose wife had carried on a year-long affair with Vel'chaninov while he lived with them in their home. She recently died of consumption, in March, the same time Vel'chaninov's peculiar "anxiety" began.

Then ensues a subtle cat-and-mouse game in which Trusotskii torments Vel'chaninov without letting on that he knows Vel'chaninov is the true father of his six-year-old daughter Liza. Finally, during a thunderstorm sometime around the end of July, Vel'chaninov wakes up in the night to find Trusotskii standing over him with an open razor. He overcomes Trusotskii and they part.

Pavel Trusotskii, "the man in mourning," is a living emanation of Vel'chaninov's conscience, much like Raskol'nikov's landlady (who is a widow) and "the lady in mourning" who quietly leaves the police station when Raskol'nikov arrives. Vel'chaninov owes Trusotskii 4000 rubles, bringing to mind the debt owed by Raskol'nikov to his landlady. Vel'chaninov's dream closely parallels that of Raskol'nikov in which Porokh beats the landlady. In one case, a symbolic Elijah the Prophet tortures the murderer's "conscience"; in the other, the transgressor fights his "conscience," which sits in judgment over him. The meek landlady peeks furtively from her room, while Trusotskii is repeatedly seen peering from small windows: the carriage window in Bagautov's funeral procession; the window of the eating establishment beside the cemetery where Liza is buried; and the little window of the upstairs room where he is locked in at the Zakhlebinins'.

After the incident with the razor, it is revealed that Trusotskii learned about his wife's affair from a letter he found soon after her death in March. Thus, Vel'chaninov's tormenting recollections of his past transgressions began at the moment his "conscience," Trusotskii, learned of his betrayal.

As an emanation of Vel'chaninov's conscience, or the divine side of his spirit, Trusotskii is repeatedly associated with Christian symbols. He refers to the hotel where he is staying as the *Pokrovskaia* ('The Intercession'). He visits women, evidently prostitutes, on *Voznesenskii* ('Ascension') *Prospekt*. When, drunk, he learns of Liza's death, he instinctively tries to cross himself. He uses the expression *kazhdyi Bozhii den'* (literally, 'on each of God's days') with a special significance when he speaks of the year when, as Vel'chaninov's host, he served him wine every day and when he mentions his daily visits to Bagautov, another one of his wife's lovers.

Numerous details suggest that Trusotskii is in a certain sense Vel'chaninov's double. Vel'chaninov wonders whether Trusotskii is spying on him or whether he himself is pursuing Trusotskii. Their close genetic relationship is intimated when Trusotskii greets Vel'chaninov as his "own brother" (*bratets rodnoi*). On their last night together, Trusotskii nurses the ailing Vel'chaninov "like his own son." Dostoevsky makes Trusotskii about seven years older than Vel'chaninov because the innocent, divine aspect of the spirit is present from birth, while the corrupt self is younger, evolving as the age of innocence passes.

Vel'chaninov complains that Trusotskii "hangs" (*visnet*) on people's necks, but he himself is forced to admit that he "depends" (*zavishu*) on Trusotskii for Liza to recover. Their unity as two symbolic halves of the human spirit is represented by their drinking together and exchanging kisses at the end of Chapter Seven. Vel'chaninov also refers to Trusotskii as a "hanger-on," using the word *visel'nik*, a term for a 'hanged man'. Together with Vel'chaninov's complaints about Trusotskii's "hanging" around his neck, this turn of speech evokes the image of a crucifix.

Vel'chaninov is inspired with the idea of making a new start in life by devoting himself heart and soul to his young daughter. In other words, without confessing his guilt to Trusotskii, he hopes to simply turn his back on the past and seek atonement in his love for Liza:

> "Liza's love," he dreamed, "would cleanse and redeem all my former useless and filthy life; instead of me, an idle, corrupt, burnt-out man, I would bring up a pure and wonderful being, and for her sake everything would be forgiven me and I would forgive myself everything." [62]

This hope is like Raskol'nikov's vow – undertaken after his talk with Marmeladov's little daughter Polechka – to embark upon a new, altruistic life without confessing his crime (Part Two, Chapter 7). The plan fails for both because, as Dostoevsky wrote in a letter to Katkov, it is contrary to "divine Truth."[6]

Liza becomes the embodiment of Vel'chaninov's projected "new self," but without Trusotskii she withers and dies. The dream of a new life is impossible without reckoning with conscience (Trusotskii) and confessing one's guilt. Liza's passing is a symbolic foreshadowing of Vel'chaninov's own spiritual death. He is haunted by a memory of "a single little finger which – God knows why – had turned black during her illness" and which he had noticed as Liza lay ready for burial. The blackened finger is the corruption of his own soul.

The expression "God knows" is placed strategically throughout the whole novel. In Chapter Two, it is used three times in the short paragraph describing Vel'chaninov's realization that the man with the crepe on his hat is the source of his anxiety:

> [...] at this moment – God knows by what process – he suddenly comprehended the reason for his anxiety, his own peculiar anxiety which had tormented him for the past several days and in general recently; God knows how it had managed to become bound to him and God knows why it did not want to be loosed; now he saw and understood everything like his own five fingers.
> "It's all that hat!" he muttered, as though inspired[...] [11]

In Chapter One, Vel'chaninov's recollections of past transgressions come "suddenly and God knows why." These seemingly insignificant turns of speech are signals that Vel'chaninov's pangs of conscience are divinely orchestrated.

After Liza's death, Vel'chaninov wanders about aimlessly for two weeks and then visits Liza's grave. At the cemetery, he is inspired with new hope and "a certain pure, peaceful faith in something" which he feels Liza has sent him from beyond the grave. The next day, he encounters Trusotskii, who now has a conciliatory expression on his face. He smells of cologne (*dukhí*) and is about to go visit the Zakhlebinins, whose youngest daughter he hopes to marry. He virtually reads Vel'chaninov's heart and mind:

> "[...] I approached you just now, basing my hopes on the nobility of certain feelings in your heart, Aleksei Ivanovich; specifically, on those very feelings which might have been awakened in your heart of late... I think I'm making myself clear, sir. Am I not?" [67]

Trusotskii persuades Vel'chaninov to accompany him on his visit to the Zakhlebinins'. The visit becomes a test to see whether Vel'chaninov can behave according to the law of God and conscience. Vel'chaninov later reminisces that Trusotskii "wanted terribly to forgive me." He analyzes Trusotskii's motives:

> "... He took me there [...] trusting in the nobility of my feelings – perhaps believing that we would embrace and weep beneath a bush there, in the proximity of innocence." [103]

But, naturally, Vel'chaninov yields to temptation and joins forces with the nihilistic "little demon" Nadya in humiliating Trusotskii.

When old Zakhlebinin leaves for his nap, he tells the young people: "God be with you, God be with you. Have fun now...." Then, in the ensuing game of proverbs, the young people use proverbs which allude to God and have a peculiar, accidental relevance to Vel'chaninov:

> "The dream is frightful, but God is merciful."

"A prayer to God and service to the Tsar will not go unrewarded." [77]

When it is Trusotskii's turn to guess the proverb, he stands waiting with his back to the group as the rules require, "intending to fulfill his sacred duty." At this moment, they make a fool of him by quietly sneaking away, leaving him to stand there alone. Later, during a game of tag, they cleverly lock him in a room upstairs. He cannot call for help because his shouts would wake up the sleeping host, and he is left to watch helplessly from the window. Symbolically, Vel'chaninov has betrayed his own conscience, allowing it to be "locked up."

By now "the hottest days of July" have set in and a thunderstorm is brewing. Like the storm itself, Trusotskii "prepares himself and concentrates" as he rides back to town with Vel'chaninov. After noticing that Trusotskii is sweating, Vel'chaninov asks the coachman:

"Will there be a thunderstorm or not?"
"There sure will! And what a storm it's going to be! It's been steamin' (*parilo*) all day!" [84]

Despite his outward good humor, Vel'chaninov experiences onslaughts of anxiety which wear him down as the day progresses. By evening he is physically ill. His suffering increases as the storm develops, reaching its peak in the middle of the night. The thunderstorm of this fateful night is once again the storm of the wrathful Elijah, which punishes unrepentant sinners. Symbolically, it is the same storm which rages when Raskol'nikov decides to confess and Svidrigailov chooses suicide.

Earlier in the day, before setting out for the Zakhlebinins', Trusotskii had promised Vel'chaninov:

"[...] when we return, I will *unfold* everything before you, like at *confession*, Aleksei Ivanovich, trust me!" [68][7]

In fact, Trusotskii *unfolds* a razor and stands over Vel'chaninov as the latter is tortured by the same dream as before. This time, however, people seem to be carrying his coffin up the stairs. Once again the bell rings three times and he wakes up, grasping the razor instinctively, without seeing it, and wresting the much weaker Trusotskii to the floor. The "unfolded" (*razvernutaia*) razor falls at his feet. He ties up Trusotskii "for some reason," locks him inside another room (again, he cannot say why), and tries to sleep again.

Before the incident with the razor, Trusotskii nurses the ailing sinner with boiling water and extremely hot plates wrapped in towels. This motif continues the fire imagery associated with Elijah. Vel'chaninov's conscience punishes him, but above all it is concerned with his spiritual welfare and salvation. "The dream is frightful, but God is merciful."

Thus, Elijah's lightning strikes and the razor unfolds over Vel'chaninov: the time for confession has come. But no confession is forthcoming. Vel'chaninov overpowers his own conscience. His tying up his "conscience" is a travesty of the sacrament of confession, known as "binding and loosing" (*sviazat' i razviazat'*).[8] When Vel'chaninov opens the room where Trusotskii is locked up, he finds his captive already untied. Trusotskii leaves, and Vel'chaninov's anxiety goes away. He feels that "something has come to an end, been resolved (*razviazalos'*: literally, 'come untied')."

After this ritual of non-confession, Vel'chaninov experiences an overwhelming urge to "tell all" (*rasskazat' vse*) to somebody, and the first person he turns to is his doctor, who earlier suggested a laxative for his anxiety. The doctor, of course, must *bind* his injured hand. In turning to the doctor, Vel'chaninov is unconsciously pursuing an inward need for confession, the sacrament of *binding and loosing.* But the need to confess is an urge which his corrupted spirit stubbornly represses.

Vel'chaninov's visit to his doctor brings to mind Goliadkin's doctor in *The Double.* Goliadkin casually compares his doctor to a priest-confessor and repeatedly stops to catch his breath (*perevesti* **dukh**) on his way to the doctor, whose name, *Krest'ian* Ivanovich, is closely associated with 'Christian.' However, the doctor has no comprehension of Goliadkin's spiritual crisis, and the author's linking him with a confessor-priest is intentionally ironical. In the end, the doctor cooperates with the world of slander and deceit in helping to relegate the good, straightforward Goliadkin Senior to an insane asylum.[9] In the same aspiritual context, Vel'chaninov tells nothing about his transgressions to his secular "confessor."

For years, Vel'chaninov has been drawn toward his friends the Pogorel'tsevs (a family name which elicits associations with *pogorel'tsy*: victims of a housefire):[10]

> Here in this family he was simple, naive and good. He took care of the children, never beat about the bush, admitted everything and confessed everything [*ispovedovalsia vo vsem*]. He swore to the Pogorel'tsevs that he would live a little longer in the "big world" and then he would move in with them for good. [39]

This pipedream is never realized.

Before going to bed on the fateful night of the storm, Trusotskii quips that he will "smoke the little spirit out of the nursery" (*My dushok etot vykurim, iz detskoi-to-s....*). He is alluding to his eighteen-year-old rival Lobov, but when Vel'chaninov wakes up in misery in the middle of the night, he has grown weak "like a baby". He notices that the storm has been raging and that the room is full of cigarette smoke (*nakureno*). It is the corruption in Vel'chaninov's spirit that Trusotskii is smoking out. His attempt at exorcism comes just as Elijah's storm is most intense. His cigarettes, like the cigarette of the fiery Il'ia Porokh, are symbolically analogous to the lightning fire of the prophet. Trusotskii began smoking in March, after his wife's death, the same time Vel'chaninov's anxiety began.[11]

The razor which Trusotskii holds over Vel'chaninov is also a parallel to the punishing lightning of Elijah, although the cut which Vel'chaninov receives comes to symbolize for him his final "divorce" from the eternal husband. Trusotskii is an "eternal husband" not only because he must always be bound to a wife, but also in that he represents the *eternal*, spiritual side of Vel'chaninov. A bond of obligation unites him with Vel'chaninov, much as it unites Raskol'nikov with his landlady. A double meaning, unknown to Vel'chaninov, is implied when he exclaims to Trusotskii: "... we are people of different worlds... a grave has come between us!" When Trusotskii replies, "Yes, but on my side there is more," the encoded message is that his side is the eternal side beyond the grave.

Two years after the fateful night, Vel'chaninov encounters Trusotskii at a provincial train station. He nearly accepts an invitation to visit Trusotskii and his new unfaithful wife at their home, but resists the temptation and chooses to continue on to see a lady friend in Odessa. The final break with his "conscience" comes when Trusotskii refuses to shake his scarred hand. By now, Vel'chaninov has learned to live a Sybarite's life of mild debauch, keeping his sins in moderation in order to avoid another duel with his conscience. After parting with Trusotskii at the end of the novel, he decides not to visit another female acquaintance who lives in the region because he is "out of spirits" (*slishkom uzh byl ne v dukhe*).

The term "conscience" (*sovest'*) is conspicuously infrequent in this tale about a man's struggle with his conscience. This is because "conscience" is the key to the allegory which the writer has constructed. It must be used sparingly for events to retain their element of mystery for both Vel'chaninov and the reader. Vel'chaninov is a worldly man who scoffs cynically at spiritual concepts. His own lack of conscience is reflected ironically in his statement to Trusotskii: "In all good conscience I consider that all affairs between us are finished." In the end, he fails to recognize his own spirituality. Raskol'nikov and Svidrigailov surrender in the struggle with their conscience; Vel'chaninov finds a *modus vivendi* which enables him to ignore his.

Studies of *The Eternal Husband* such as the eighty-page treatise by V.Ia. Kirpotin which approach the work only as a realistic portrayal of peculiar psychological types tend to miss the point. Kirpotin, for example, writes nothing about the spiritual significance of the storm, the relevance to Vel'chaninov of "smoking out the spirit," the connection between the razor and confession, and the many word-plays and casual allusions which are guideposts to theme at the deepest level. One can only assume that he has overlooked these important features.[12]

Dostoevskii's lively, masterful portrayal of human behavior should not blind one to the movements of the spirit which outward behavior so often reflects in his works. In characters such as Raskol'nikov's landlady and Trusotskii, the symbolic creatures of medieval allegory are bestowed with the flesh and blood of modern realism. Dostoevsky's technique is one of symbolic realism in which *symbolic* and *realistic* elements are dispersed unevenly throughout his various works. Some of his lesser known works, such as *The Landlady, Stepanchikovo* and *The Eternal Husband*, owe their relative obscurity to the fact that in them allegory – often unnoticed by the reader – tends to outweigh realism, in contrast to more popular novels such as *Crime and Punishment* and *The Brothers Karamazov*, where a more explicit realistic style tends to prevail.

NOTES

Introduction: Elijah the Prophet in Russian Tradition

1 See A.N. Afanas'ev, *Poeticheskie vozzreniia slavian na prirodu* (3 vols., Moscow, 1865-690), vol.1, pp.469-83, 628, 630, 640, 698, 737, 762.
2 Cited from Ivan Turgenev, *Fathers and Sons*, ed. Ralph E. Matlaw, Norton, New York, 1966, p.39 [Chapter 10].
3 N.A. Goncharov, *Sobranie sochinenii v shesti tomakh*, vol.4, Moscow, 1972, p.104 [my translation].
4 See Robert Mann, *Oral Composition in the Old Russian Igor Tale*, doctoral dissertation, University of Kansas, 1984, chapter 1, pp.17-66.
5 See *ibid*. For an English translation of the Igor Tale with a brief 40-page commentary, see Robert Mann, *The Song of Prince Igor*, Vernyhora Press, Eugene, 1979 [Coronado Press: Lawrence, Kansas].
6 See V.V. Ivanov, V.N. Toporov, *Issledovaniia v oblasti slavianskikh drevnostei. Leksicheskie i frazeologicheskie voprosy rekonstruktsii tekstov*, Moscow, 1974.
7 *Polnoe sobranie russkikh letopisei*, vol.3, Petersburg, 1841, p.207.
8 Cited with alterations from Mann, *The Song of Prince Igor*, p.15.
9 See Mann, *Oral Composition*, pp.162-67; *The Song of Prince Igor*, pp.35-36.
10 See Afanas'ev, *Poeticheskie vozzreniia*; Ivanov, Toporov, *Issledovaniia*, Mann, *Oral Composition*, chapter 2, pp.67-90.
11 Dimit"r and Konstantin Miladinovtsi, *B"lgarski narodni pesni*, 4th ed., Sofija, 1961, no.31, 38; Afanas'ev, *Poeticheskie vozzreniia*, vol.1, pp.642-44.
12 *Ibid.*
13 Mann, *Oral Composition*, p.68.
14 See Afanas'ev, *Poeticheskie vozzreniia*, vol.1, pp.560-61.
15 *Velikii sbornik*, chast' 2 (*Mineia prazdnichnaia*), 2nd ed., Jordanville, 1954, p.181.
16 See Mann, *Oral Composition*, chapter 1, esp. pp.28-30.
17 *Polnoe sobranie russkikh letopisei*, vol.1, Leningrad, 1926,

    p.54.
18 See Mann, *Oral Composition*, chapter 2; *The Song of Prince Igor*, pp.15, 22, 37-39, 53-55.
19 See P.F. Hlebka, I.V. Hutarav, *Belaruski epas*, Minsk, 1959, p.56.
20 See Mann, *Oral Composition*, chapter 1, note 24.
21 *Ibid.*, pp.25-33.
22 See *Literaturnoe nasledstvo*, vol.77 (*F.M. Dostoevskii v rabote nad romanom "Podrostok". Tvorcheskie rukopisi*), ed. I.I. Anisimov, Moscow, 1965, pp.388, 389, 368-69, 357. I am indebted to James L. Rice (University of Oregon) for pointing out to me these important passages.
23 See F.M. Dostoevskii, *Polnoe sobranie sochinenii v tridtsati tomakh*, Leningrad, 1972- (hereafter *PSS*), vol.20, p.189; vol.22, pp.153, 161; vol.24, pp.169, 309.

Part One: Crime and Punishment

1. See Georgii Meier, *Svet v nochi (o "Prestuplenii i nakazanii). Opyt medlennogo chteniia*, Frankfurt/Main, 1967.
2. All citations from the final version of *Crime and Punishment* are identified by page number in *PSS*, volume 6 (1973). English translations and italics are my own.
3. The juxtaposition of "crosses" and "crossroads" in the following passage highlights the symbolic connection between the crossroads and the cross: "...I've come for your crosses, Sonia. After all, it was you who sent me to the crossroads..." [403].
4. *PSS*, vol.7 (1973), p.192.
5. Mary Magdalene came from Magdal, a town *near Capernaum*, as noted by the editors in *PSS*, vol.7, pp.365-66.
6. Georgii Meier notes the parallel between the name Il'ia and the Biblical Elijah, but he misses the word-play between *prorok* and *porokh*. See Meier, *Svet v nochi*, pp.43-45. A prototype for Il'ia Petrovich "Porokh" in real life was a policeman who helped Dostoevskii when he was threatened with jail for nonpayment of debts in June, 1865. See *PSS*, vol.7, p.370.

Petr Il'ich Perkhotin, to whom Dmitrii Karamazov pawns his pistols, also has associations with Elijah the Prophet. His name, *Perkhotin*, seems to be a reminiscence of *Porokh* in *Crime and Punishment*. Powder is mentioned along with the pistols themselves when Dmitrii goes to Perkhotin to reclaim the pistols, contemplating suicide. [Book 8, Part 5] Dmitrii's obtaining the pistols is paralleled by Kolia Krasotkin's trading a book for a miniature cannon. In Book 10, Kolia gives the cannon, together with gunpowder and shot, to the dying boy Iliusha, who lies in his corner beneath the icons. Along with the cannon, Kolia gives Iliusha the dog *Perezvon*, whose name signifies the peal of church bells (an old Slavic name, Kolia emphasizes). At this point, Kolia is about to turn away from the rationalistic, socialist ideas represented in part by Rakitin, gravitating instead to the Christian example of Alesha Karamazov. The cannon symbolizes the fire of Elijah which the atheists and revolutionaries have usurped. In giving the cannon to Iliusha, Kolia is symbolically surrendering the fire to Elijah in the person of the Prophet's namesake as he is about to ascend into heaven.

There is a peculiar, church-like aura to Iliusha's home with its "uncommon quietness," its Russian stove and Iliusha's bed beneath the icons – suggestive of a special symbolic significance which the author sees in Iliusha and his family. Iliusha's father, a red-haired former army captain named Nikolai *Il'ich*, speaks with a tinge of irony when he calls his home *khoromy* ('palace chambers,' but suggestive of *khram* 'temple'). He calls his daughter "an angel of God in the flesh," and a topic of conversation during Alesha's visit is the stuffiness of the air. (See below concerning the symbolic function of words derived from *dukh*.) Nikolai Il'ich's flying a kite (*zmei*: 'kite,' 'dragon') with his son Iliusha brings to mind the struggle of Elijah with the beast of the Apocalypse (a dragon, according to one ancient source) as well as a similar apocalyptic kite motif in *Stepanchikovo*. (See Part 2.)

In obtaining the pistols from Perkhotin, Dmitrii is symbolically usurping the Prophet's fire, continuing along an un-Christian path of passion and violence. Perkhotin, it should be noted, is a positive hero who defeats Rakitin in a protracted duel of wit and will. The book which Kolia trades for the cannon is entitled *Mohammed's Kinsman*, while Mohammed has symbolic associations with Elijah in Dostoevsky's fiction (based on at least two factors: both are Prophets and both rise into heaven and witness the light of Truth). The bag in which Kolia keeps the gunpowder is referred to as a *puzyrek* ('bag,' 'bladder,' 'bubble'). In the same section [Book 10, Part 2], Kolia calls the children who have been left in his care *puzyri* ('bubbles'). Dostoevsky seems to be intimating that the children are potential vessels for the incendiary creeds of revolutionaries. Iliusha's symbolic connection with Elijah the Prophet was first noted by James Rice in *Dostoevsky and the Healing Art: An Essay in Literary and Medical History*, Ardis, Ann Arbor, 1985, pp.270-71.

Other word-plays in *Crime and Punishment* worth noting

include Il'ia Petrovich's mistaken reference to Svidrigailov as *Nil Pavlych* immediately after speaking of nihilists and using the Latin *nihil est* in his characterization of Raskol'nikov [407-8]. This word-play shows that the author saw a second meaning in Svidrigailov's quotation from Terence: "I am also human *et nihil humanum...*" [215]. The secondary allusion is to Svidrigailov's own nihilism. Another example is the name of the building in which Raskol'nikov formerly lived. Razumikhin's phrasing results in a variation on *obukha dom* ('the house of the blunt end of the axehead'): "[...] I looked and looked for this Kharlam's house, and then it turned out that it wasn't Kharlam's house at all, but Bukh's [*a Bukha*]. The way one gets confused with sounds sometimes!..." [96]

7   I wish to thank Anthony Anemone (University of California at Berkeley), who first pointed out to me the name of the Church of Elijah the Prophet at the Powderworks. Located on Leningrad's *Shosse revoliutsii*, the dilapidated 18th-century church is now in the early stages of restoration.

8   I.A. Goncharov, *Sobranie sochinenii v shesti tomakh*, vol.4, Moscow, 1972, pp.391, 310. The annual excursions to the powderworks are also mentioned in Part 4, Chapter 6 (p.454) and Part 4, Chapter 9 (p.494). Elijah's feast day is alluded to repeatedly in *Oblomov* (pp.104, 130, 133, 402, 408, 441), usually in conjunction with the nameday of the central character, *Il'ia Il'ich* Oblomov. The theme of Judgment for Oblomov's life of idleness continues throughout the whole novel, and allusions to thunder and lightning suggest that Oblomov's death comes as divine retribution for a sinful way of living. (Compare p.493: "He inwardly rejoiced that he had escaped its [life's] annoying, tortuous demands and storms – that horizon where the lightning of great joys flashes and the sudden blows [*udary*] of great sorrows resound [...]" and pp.494-495: "In the summer they would go outside of town, and on Elijah's Friday they would go to the Powderworks, and life proceeded in its usual way. And if it were true that life's blows [*udary*] never reach any peaceful little corners, then one could even say that there were no disastrous changes. Unfortunately, however, when the thunder's

blow [*udar*] shakes the mountains and the vast heavenly expanses, it is also heard in the mouse's burrow. Although it is weaker and somewhat muted, it is still quite audible in the burrow." Then Oblomov is felled by an apoplectic stroke (*apopleksicheskii* ***udar***), whereupon he is told that he must change his way of living. Later the stroke recurs and he soon dies.) Oblomov has idled away thirty-two or thirty-three years at the beginning of the novel and is now expected to accomplish deeds. Goncharov has in mind the epic hero Il'ia Muromets (Elijah of Murom), who sits paralyzed for thirty-three years before accomplishing great feats. In Oblomov's case, however, no feats materialize. The author hints at the connection by referring to Oblomov as a *dobryi molodets* ('good lad': a folkloric formula used most commonly with epic heroes) and then alluding to Il'ia Muromets and the Pilgrim Ivan a few paragraphs later [120-21].

9   *PSS*, vol.7, p.17.
10 The original Russian reads: "*nabrosilsia vsemi perunami*" [78].
11 *Smerch*, a term for a whirlwind, tornado or waterspout is used instead of *vikhr'*: "*Opiat' grokhot, opiat' grom i molniia, smerch, uragan!* " [79].
12 Meier, op. cit.
13 Meier also notes that the silent "woman in mourning" (*traurnaia dama*) who leaves the police station soon after Raskol'nikov arrives is another emanation of Raskol'nikov's conscience, or the godly aspect of his spirit. See Meier, pp.153-56.
14 Raskol'nikov's German attributes were inherited in part from Pushkin's Germann. See A. Bem, "Gogol' i Pushkin v tvorchestve Dostoevskogo," *Slavia*, VII, 1928-1929, pp.63-86; VIII, 1929-1930, pp.82-100, 297-311. Concerning the symbolic connection between Raskol'nikov's hat and the ideas inside his head, compare the allusions to his hat on pp.7, 101 and 407.
15 See James L. Rice, "Raskol'nikov and Tsar Gorox," *Slavic and East European Journal*, 25, no.3 (Fall 1981), pp.38-53.
16 Compare the German brothel keeper's repetition of "noble house" (*blagorodnyi dom*) with the German landlady's chatter about "noble ladies" ("*blagorodnyi dam*").

17 Meier (p.44) links the landlady with Raskol'nikov's own soul, which he has given over to torments. Meier does not note the symbolism of the landlady's name.
18 Zarnitsyna's first name and patronymic are *Praskov'ia Pavlovna* in the final version [26]. (See Part 2 on St. Paraskevna.) In one of the notebooks they are *Iuliia Prokhorovna*, which mirrors *Iliia Porokh*. (See *PSS*, vol.7, p.153.) Raskol'nikov had been concerned for the landlady's invalid daughter and intended to marry her. In a sense, she was the "daughter" of his own conscience, symbolized by Zarnitsyna.
19 A term for such realizations, or illuminations, of conscience is *ozarenie*, which shares the same root with *zarnitsa* and *zaria* ('dawn'). The landlady in the early story *The Landlady* also symbolizes the central character's soul and is closely linked with the dawn in the imagery of the story. See Part 4.
20 The verb "*ozaril*" ('illuminated') is intended to elicit associations with *ozarenie* and *zarnitsa*. See note 16.
21 In the early stages of writing *Crime and Punishment* (September, 1865) Dostoevskii stated in a letter to Katkov that Raskol'nikov passes "almost a month" before confessing. See Konstantin Mochulsky, *Dostoevsky: His Life and Work*, (transl. Michael A. Minihan) Princeton, 1967, pp.272-73. The rainstorm which begins just before the arrest of Dmitrii Karamazov also has symbolic associations with Elijah. An intimation of this is Dmitrii's speaking of the "thunder" which has struck him. The name of the village where the storm finds Dmitrii – *Mokroe*: literally, 'Wet' – is intended to highlight the symbolic significance of the storm. A certain "Il'inskii father" (a priest from a village named after Elijah) previously leads Dmitrii to a village called *Sukhoi Poselok* ('Dry Settlement'): "...*batiushka soglasilsia, odnako, provodit' ego v Sukhoi Poselok, no na grekh posovetoval idti peshechkom...*" [Book 8, Part 2] Fyodr Karamazov says of the priest: "...he's a man of gold, but he can't see to anything, as though he weren't a man at all..." [Book 5, Part 7]. Cf. Nikodim Fomich's allusion to "the gold of Porokh's heart."
22 *PSS*, vol.7, p.149. See also pp.134-35, 137, 139 and 143.

23 *Ibid.*, p.148.
24 Compare Prokharchin's vision of Judgment during a housefire (discussed in Part 3] and the apocalyptic experience of Stepan Trofimovich after the fire in *The Possessed* (examined in Chapter Two). Also note Dmitrii Karamazov's dream about the fire victims, coupled with the symbolism of the rainstorm [*The Brothers Karamazov*, Book 8, Part 8; Book 11, Part 1].
25 The genitive of *vino* ('wine,' 'spirits') is a homonym of *vina* ('guilt'). It is this homonym which Dostoevskii employs here: *s vina*.
26 *PSS*, vol.7, pp.377.
27 *Ibid.*
28 The usurper motif is prominent in *The Village of Stepanchikovo and Its Inhabitants.* (See Part 2.) In *The Brothers Karamazov*, Adam and Prometheus coalesce when man's fall is characterized as an attempt to usurp the divine fire. In Part Two, Book 5, Chapter 4, Ivan says, "I'm only an insect and I confess in all humility that I can't understand at all why everything is arranged this way. It turns out that people are guilty themselves: paradise was given to them, but they wanted freedom and stole the fire from heaven, knowing they'd be unhappy."
29 The Biblical cup motif is also employed in *A Nasty Story* (*PSS*, vol.5 [1973], pp.37-38): "Finally she gave him her own money, but forced Pseldonimov to drink such a cup of gall and vinegar that he tore at his hair in silence and flung himself on the bed... trembling from impotent rage." Like Raskol'nikov, Dmitrii Karamazov is urged to drink a cup of water when he is arrested [Book 9, Part 3] He sees his path to atonement as the path of Christ, as shown by his talk of "suffering," "crucifixion" and "tomorrow's cross" in Book 11, Part 4.
30 Raskol'nikov fears Svidrigailov as a potential *betrayer*. Svidrigailov is the only person with evidence of the murderer's identity and might report. Raskol'nikov and Sonia also enter Judas' path (Sonia sells herself the first time for thirty rubles; Raskol'nikov virtually sells his soul in a nihilistic scheme to obtain 3,000 rubles), but they turn from the path of Judas to that of Christ. When Judas hanged himself, he left the money in the

sanctuary, and the priests used it to buy a field for a graveyard (Matthew 27:5-10). Before committing suicide, Svidrigailov pays for Katerina Ivanovna's funeral and leaves money for the Marmeladovs' orphans.

31 See Part 1, Book 3, Chapter 11 of *The Brothers Karamazov*. Also note the symbolic link between the *rakita* bush and the Judaizer *Rakitin* (nicknamed "*Rakitka*"), who delivers Alesha to Grushenka for a 25-ruble credit note and then tells Alesha: "... you're not Christ and I'm not Judas." [Book 7, Chapter 4] The author is hinting that Rakitin *is* like Judas; hence, the name *Rakitin*, associated with the bush on which Judas hanged himself.

32 See G.A. Brokgauz, I.A. Efron, *Entsiklopedicheskii slovar'*, vol.24, Petersburg, 1898, p.334. See also Evgenii Sarukhanian, *Dostoevskii v Peterburge*, Leningrad, 1972, p.192. The Jewish fireman is said to have a sorrowful expression like that of *all* Jews without exception. He tells Raskol'nikov in a thick accent: "This is not the place."

33 The text does not state explicitly that the spoon is silver, but it must doubtless be silver if it has any value for the Jew who takes it. Note also the peculiar significance of silver spoons to the Marmeladovs' German landlady [V, 3] (a parallel that was pointed out to me by Scott Filar at Knox College). Her name, incidentally, – Lippewechsel – sounds like "false receipt" in Russian (*lipa* 'fake' and *veksel'* 'receipt' [from German]), a most humorous name for a landlady.

34 The term "finger of God" (*palets Bozhii*) once referred throughout Slavdom to elongated stones resembling stalactites which were found in the ground and attributed in pagan times to the thunder god. In *The Brothers Karamazov* Nikolai Il'ich says that Iliusha is his only son – "alone, like a finger."

35 Sarukhanian, *pp.185-89*.

36 Compare the associations between epilepsy (*paduchaia* 'the falling sickness') and man's fall in *The Landlady* and *The Idiot*, discussed in Part 4. *Pripadok* is used in reference to Smerdiakov's presumed epileptic attack in *The Brothers Karamazov*. Also note the lightning imagery in *Crime and Punishment*, pp.193, 196 and 251.

37 See Mochulsky, op.cit., p.312.
38 *Ibid.*
39 *PSS*, vol.7, p.203.

Part Two: *The Village of Stepanchikovo* and *The Possessed*

1. *PSS*, vol.3 (1972), pp.5-168. *Stepanchikovo* was first published, serially, in *Notes of the Fatherland* (1859, no.11, 12). English translations are my own.
2. *PSS*, vol.10 (1974). *The Possessed* was first published, serially, in 1871-72.
3. The name *Perepelitsyna* is from *perepelitsa* (more common form: *perepelka*): 'quail'. Perepelitsyna flutters and squawks like a quail in a storm.
4. *Stolby* ('pillars') is a term for the Northern Lights. The term *stolb* ('pillar') as well as *stolbniak* ('stupor') and *ostolbenet'* ('to be stupefied,' literally: 'to turn into a pillar') are repeatedly applied to Rostanev. See, for example, pages 23, 55, 56, 57 and 84. Rostanev's blinking his eyes as he stands like a "pillar" is suggestive of a distant, benign lightning display.
5. The original reads: "*Naruzhnosti on byl bogatyrskoi...*"
6. See Introduction.
7. The wandering pilgrim Ivanishche also figures in Dostoevsky's notes. See *PSS*, vol.20 (1980), p.189; vol.22 (1981), pp.153, 161; vol.24 (1982), pp.169, 309. For Il'ia Muromets in *A Little Hero* (published 1857), see *PSS*, vol.2 (1972), pp. 282-86.
8. A curious coincidence worth noting is the reference to Foma as an "idol," while the foes of Il'ia Muromets are the Huge Idol and his henchmen.
9. The walking stick shows that Foma's earlier tirade about Rostanev's mother taking a walking stick and going begging is actually a foreshadowing of Foma's own trek through the "lake" of rain.
10. Rostanev replies to his nephew: "Wondrous and amazing is the Creator!" [*Divnyi, divnyi Tvorets!*] Viewed together with the nephew's comments, these words closely parallel the sentence which Dostoevsky planned at one point to employ at the very end of *Crime and Punishment*: "Wondrous are the paths by which God will find a man." [*Neispovedimy puti, kotorymi*

nakhodit Bog cheloveka.] *PSS*, vol.7, p.203

11 Later in the novel [71], Egor relates how he was once allowed to ask a question at an oral examination. He asked, "Who was Noah?"

12 Other hints at Rostanev's role as a symbolic manifestation of God include allusions to his wrath. With typical humility, Egor says that he knows little about science and "only hears that they're ringing on the next bell tower" [48]. This passage is densely packed with words that are suggestive of the underlying religious allegory: *kaius'* (literally, 'I repent'); "What, my little soul?"; "Oh, my God!"; "Forgive me, for Christ's sake!" As the narrator journeys from Petersburg to Stepanchikovo and the countryside unfolds before him, it seems to him that "only now was he getting to see God's world after being couped up in Petersburg." [19]

13 See Dmitry Likhachov, Vera Laurina, Vasily Pushkariov, *Novgorod Icons. 12th-17th Century*, Aurora, Leningrad, 1980. Plate 75 shows Sts. Nicholas, Paraskeva, Blaise and Elijah on a two-part icon; plate 79 shows Paraskeva and Anastasia beside Barlaam of Khutyn and John the Almsgiver; plate 89 shows an icon with only Paraskeva and Anastasia; plate 214 shows Paraskeva and Anastasia with Nicholas and John the Almsgiver; plate 92 shows Elijah, Nicholas and Anastasia.

14 See Felix Hause, *Volksglaube und Brauchtum der Ostslaven* [in: *Wort und Brauch, Volkskundliche Arbeiten namens der Schlesischen Gesellschaft für Volkskunde*, no.26 (Breslau, 1939), pp.183-85.

15 See A.N. Afanas'ev, *Poeticheskie vozzreniia slavian na prirodu* (3 vols., Petersburg, 1865-69), vol.1, pp. 232-37; Leonid Ouspensky, Vladimir Lossky, *The Meaning of Icons*, St. Vladimir's Academy, Crestwood, 1982, p.136.

16 See Afanas'ev, op. cit.

17 *Ibid.*

18 *Ibid.*, vol.1, pp. 248, 263; V.V. Ivanov, V.N. Toporov, *Issledovaniia v oblasti slavianskikh drevnostei*, Institut Slavianovedeniia i Balkanistiki, Moscow, 1974, pp.24-29. In Russia, Paraskeva's feast day is October 28.

19 See note 13.
20 See Afanas'ev, vol.1 (1865), pp.699-712.
21 Another character who runs amuck morally is Obnoskin. His error is to attempt to *carry off* Tat'iana Ivanovna. His name is derived from *nosit'* ('to carry'). Compare: *Opiskin* and *Obnoskin*.
22 See Robert Mann, *Oral Composition in the Slovo o polku Igoreve*, doctoral dissertation, University of Kansas, 1984, pp. 67-77.
23 See Part Four.
24 The original Russian refers to *Khariinskaia pustosh'*. *Pustosh'* is a term for a field that has been neglected or allowed to "go to seed." It elicits associations with *opustoshit'* and is vaguely suggestive of a wasteland. *Khariinskaia* seems to be a truncated corruption of *Zakhariin* ('Zacharias's'), referring to one of the Old Testament prophets of apocalyptic doom. The allusion seems to be to "Zacharias' wasteland," a subtle signal of an imminent apocalyptic cataclysm.
25 See, for example, Russian editions of Revelation 14-15.
26 Foma brags that he has ignited "a spark of divine fire" in Rostanev [16-17]. He has in mind the flame of knowledge and culture. To the reader, however, it is entirely clear that Foma is an imposter. The "divine fire" is firmly in the possession of Egor Il'ich, as becomes clear when he finally explodes. Foma also boasts that he once donated all his pay to state education and to *fire victims* in Kazan' [16]. He himself is a "fire victim" of sorts, and he is doubtless lying. In his prophet's pose, Foma "flares up like gunpowder" [16], but – in the words of the nephew – Rostanev eventually "grinds him to powder" [*steret' v poroshok*: 114, 115].
27 See A.N. Afanas'ev, *Narodnye russkie skazki* (3 vols., Moscow, 1957), vol.1, no.164: "Koz'ma Skorobogatyi."
28 The servant says that Bakhcheev could have brought Malan'ia with him. He is being ironical, but his statement is part of the allegorical network. Like Porfirii Petrovich in *Crime and Punishment*, who is associated with Elijah, although not as thoroughly as Il'ia Porokh, Bakhcheev stands in Rostanev's

shadow as a secondary manifestation of Elijah. He is continually enraged and his stern love for his servants and peasants parallels that of Egor Il'ich. The allusion to Malan'ia travelling with Bakhcheev in his four-horse carriage elicits associations with the prophet racing in his four-horse chariot with lightning (*molon'ia*) in hand.

29 See *PSS*, vol.3, pp. 499-500, 505-506.
30 *Ibid.*, p.505.
31 *Ibid.*
32 *Ibid.*, pp. 505-507.
33 The merchant as a symbol of God will be dealt with below.
34 The insignia on Russian police and fire wagons should be identified in order to correctly evaluate this motif.
35 "Ivan Filippovich" appears to be a blend of Ivan Czarevich and Danilo Filippov, the founder of the Khlyst sect who called himself Sabaoth. He was active throughout the second half of the seventeenth century and died in 1700. See *Entsiklopedicheskii slovar'*, vol.35, Brokgauz, Efron, Petersburg, 1902, p.757.
36 Other casual turns of speech pointing to Stepan's pilgrimage as a symbolic journey to Judgment include: "He became so embarrassed that he wanted to rise and leave the hut. [...] He turned to her with the gesture of a man saving himself and offered her some tea." [488] When Stepan is told that the steamer to Spasov will arrive the next afternoon: "*Mais qu'est que ce qu'il a cet homme ?*" Stepan shuddered, awaiting his fate with fright."

Part Three: "Mr. Prokharchin"

1 *PSS*, vol.1, pp.240-63.
2 See *ibid.*, pp.502-506.
3 *Ibid.*, p.502.
4 See, for example, Victor Terras, *The Young Dostoevsky (1846-1849). A Critical Study*, Mouton, The Hague, 1969, p.267: "*Gospodin Prokharchin* is the irreverent, cynical, nihilistic treatment of a serious theme..."; Victor Terras, "The Young Dostoevsky: an Assessment in Light of Recent Scholarship" [in *New Essays on Dostoevsky*, ed. Malcolm V. Jones, Garth M. Terry, Cambridge University Press, Cambridge, 1983], p.37: "It seems likely that the young Dostoevsky was secularly oriented and disinclined to undertake the incursions into the realm of metaphysics which characterize the mature writer."
5 See A. Bem [Boehme], "Gogol' i Pushkin v tvorchestve Dostoevskogo," *Slavia*, VII, 1928-29, pp.63-86; VIII, 1929-30, pp.82-100, 297-311.
6 See *PSS*, vol.1, p.503.
7 The symbolism of the name *Sud'bin* is intimated by conspicuous repetition of the word *sud'ba* in the paragraph preceding the account of Sud'bin's search for Prokharchin [246].
8 Coming soon after the allusion to five-kopek coins (*piataki*), the expression "lifting his heels" (*podbiraia piatki*) seems to be an intentional pun. It elicits associations with *podbiraia piataki* ('picking up five-kopek pieces'). After all, Prokharchin is saving money as he runs and kicks up his heels.
9 See, for example, T.V. Tolstaya, *The Assumption Cathedral of the Moscow Kremlin*, Moscow, 1979, plate 99. Concerning apocalyptic motifs, one should also note that "the bald one" (*lysyi*) is a colloquialism for the Devil in Russian. The bald office worker who speaks of his seven children makes Prokharchin feel guilty and threatened (foreshadowing the Last Judgment). The housefire is rumored to have been caused by a baldheaded old woman.
10 The term *predstavlenie* ('presentation') here elicits associations with *predstat'* ('to present oneself'; e.g., before the Creator) and

perhaps with *svetoprestavlenie* ('end of the world').

11 Compare the close association between the landlady Zarnitsyna (derived from the word for 'sheet lightning') and the lightning wielder Il'ia Porokh. (See Part 1.) Also note the amorous attraction between Zarnitsyna and Razumikhin, who helps to guide Raskol'nikov onto a moral path.

12 Concerning Dostoevsky's use of the term *kondrashka* in connection with his own epileptic seizures, see James L. Rice, *Dostoevsky and the Healing Art*, Ardis, 1984, pp.5-10, 57. The importance of Dostoevsky's epilepsy for his fiction is immense. See Rice, esp. pp.1-111. Concerning the symbolic associations between the "falling sickness" and the fall of man, and Dostoevsky's creative treatment of an epileptic seizure as a flash of divine light, see also Part 4 below.

13 See Harry B. Weber's excellent article "*Pikovaja dama*: A Case for Freemasonry in Russian Literature," *Slavic and East European Journal*, vol.XII, No.4 (1968), pp.435-47.

14 Dostoevsky alludes to poems by Derzhavin (written in 1794) in comparing Prokharchin's mattress to the nest of a swallow (*domovitaia lastochka*). In Derzhavin's poetry, this swallow symbolizes the soul of the poet's late wife. Her soul is compared to the swallow as it opens its eyes and rises in the springtime. The poem ends with this stanza:

> My soul! You are a guest in this world:
> Is this plumed one not you?
> Sing of eternal life, my lyre!
> I shall rise, I too shall rise –
> I shall rise, – and in the ether's abyss
> Will I see you, Plenira?

The suggestion of Prokharchin's "rising" after death might be a tongue-in-cheek, ironical allusion to the rising soul in Derzhavin's verse. See G.R. Derzhavin, *Stikhotvoreniia*, Leningrad, 1981, pp.98-100.

15 Note the repetition in this paragraph of the name *Semyon*, which echoes the number "seven" (*sem'*).

16 *Tuz* has the secondary meaning 'bigshot' in colloquial Russian. The primary meaning of *shut* is 'jester.' I have taken the liberty

of translating it here in its secondary, implied meaning, 'Joker.' In *Stepanchikovo*, Dostoevsky toys once again with the associations between "Joker" and the Devil: the old general "even wept out of anger and exasperation, all because of nothing more than some Jack [*valet*] which was played instead of a Nine. Eventually, because of his poor eyesight, he needed a reader. That's when Foma Fomich Opiskin appeared." [7] [Foma serves the general as a virtual valet.] A few sentences later, Foma is described in his role as the general's jester (*shut*).

17 Russian schoolchildren use *kol* as a term for a failing grade of "one."
18 The later *Stepanchikovo* seems to contain a reminiscence of this motif in a passage which comes soon after the characterization of Foma Fomich as a "jester": "Foma surmised what sort of man he now faced [Rostanev], and immediately had the feeling that his jester's role had passed and, for lack of other candidates, Foma himself could be one of the gentry [*dvorianin*, also, literally, 'a member of the royal court']."

Part Four: *The Landlady* and *The Idiot*

1 Cited from Dostoevskii, *PSS*, vol.1, p.510.
2 See A.L. Bem, "Dramatizatsiia breda ('Khoziaika' Dostoevskogo)," *Dostoevskii. Psikhoanaliticheskie etiudy*, Berlin, 1938 [Reprint by Ardis, 1983], pp.77-141; R. Neuhäuser, "'The Landlady.' A New Interpretation," *Canadian Slavonic Papers*, vol.X, no.1 (1968), pp.42-67.
3 See *PSS*, vol.1, p.508; Neuhäuser.
4 *The Landlady* is cited from *PSS*, vol.1. English translations are my own. Italicized words serve to indicate my own emphasis and are not graphically marked in the original Russian.
5 See note 4.
6 In *The Idiot*, Myshkin speaks rapturously about "God's sunset" (*Bozhiia zaria*) immediately before his epileptic seizure at the Epanchins' (IV, 7). The mystical associations of celestial light will be discussed briefly below.
7 For a bibliography of recorded texts of this epic song see A.M. Astakhova, *Il'ia Muromets*, Moscow and Leningrad, 1958, p.471; P.D. Ukhov, *Byliny*, Moscow, 1957, pp.455-56.
8 See the many descriptions of the Russian folk wedding ritual in P.V. Kireevskii, *Pesni, sobrannye P.V. Kireevskim* [novaia seriia, Obshchestvo Liubitelei Rossiiskoi Slovesnosti pri Imperatorskom Moskovskom Universitete], 1911-1929.
9 As Bem has noted, the outlines of Dostoevsky's later theme of The Grand Inquisitor are discernible in *The Landlady*. The theme of bread versus freedom, hinted at in *The Landlady* in this proverb, is developed more elaborately in *The Brothers Karamazov* (Book 2, Part 5): "...for nothing was ever more unbearable for man and human society than freedom! Do you see these stones in this scorched, naked desert? Turn them into bread, and mankind will follow you like a grateful and obedient flock, although they will forever tremble at the thought that you might draw back your hand and their bread will come to an end."
10 See *Kniga zhitii sviatykh*, Moscow, 1840, pp.131-34; *PSS*, vol.1, p.509. The word *murin* is also a little known term for a devil. However, in Ordynov's symbolic delirium, any hellish

associations which Il'ia Murin might have are with the Devil in his fierce, punishing aspect (like Elijah the Prophet), not really the tempter. The first name of Ordynov's old landlady at the beginning of the story is Domna, also a term for a furnace. Like the Russian stove in the story, this name is suggestive of the Fiery Furnace and Ordynov's guilt. Tatar motifs in *The Landlady* are evocative of Hell, partly through associations with *Tartar*, the classical term for the underworld (Tartarus), and similar Russian words such as *tartarary*. Murin, for example, speaks Tatar with Katerina's mother (the grammar of sin and guilt, incomprehensible to the young Katerina before her liaison with Murin), and a Tatar janitor stands outside Murin's entryway, where a coffinmaker lives. Ordynov's name is derived from *orda* ('horde,' associated primarily with the Tatar hordes) and, hence, alludes to his sinful, fallen condition.

11 See V.N. Lazarev, *Stranitsy istorii novgorodskoi zhivopisi. Pages from the History of Novgorod Painting*, Moscow, 1977, plate XXIII-B.
12 Compare Dostoevsky's description of a limited, one-dimensional German (with his steadfast wife Minchen) in his *Petersburg Chronicle* (1847): *PSS*, vol.18, pp.29-34. Also note his insistence on the *sinfulness* of the lifestyle of the "Petersburg dreamer" (closely related to Ordynov).
13 See Neuhäuser and note 10.

Part Five: The Eternal Husband

1. See *PSS*, vol. 9 (1974), p.482.
2. See *Sankt-Peterburgskie vedomosti*, 1870, January 31, No.31; *PSS*, vol. 9, pp.482-83.
3. See *Golos*, 1870, March 20, No.79; *PSS*, vol. 9, p.482.
4. From a letter to Strakhov dated March 30/18, 1869. Cited from V.Ia. Kirpotin, *Mir Dostoevskogo. Etiudy i issledovaniia*, Moscow, 1980, p.169.
5. Trusotskii, on the other hand, embodies traditional "feminine" traits: physical weakness, emotionality, faith, devotion etc. In addition to the female characters representing Raskol'nikov's conscience, there is also the tradesman whose face is reminiscent of a peasant woman. He stalks Raskol'nikov as another emanation of his conscience. *The Eternal Husband* is cited throughout this chapter from *PSS*, vol.9, pp.5-112. English translations and italics are my own.
6. See *PSS*, vol.7, pp.310-11; 154-55.
7. The original reads: "*A potom, kogda priedem obratno, ia vse razvernu pered vami kak na ispovedi. Aleksei Ivanovich, dover'tes'!*" [Chapter 11]
8. The term "binding and loosing" can be traced to Matthew 16:17-19; 18:18. It is commonly used in the writings of the Russian Orthodox Church. See, for example, the *Trebnik*. Note the passage cited earlier in which Vel'chaninov's anxiety is said to be "bound" to him and will not be "loosed". In a draft, Trusotskii taunts Vel'chaninov with the idea of having their case judged in court, where he would simply claim that they had been drunk and were fighting over a prostitute. Vel'chaninov fears any public exposure. (See *PSS*, vol.10, p.304.) Trusotskii's "hanging" on Vel'chaninov's neck is vaguely suggestive of binding; i.e., the bonds of conscience. The Grand Inquisitor refers to loosing and binding in *The Brothers Karamazov* [Book 5, Part 5]. Also compare: "*...on edinyi sviazal menia, i sudiia moi...*" [Book 6, Part 2].
9. Goliadkin's encounters with his doctor serve as a framing device, like Vel'chaninov's visits to his doctor. See *PSS*, vol.1 (1972),

pp.109-229.
10 The role of the Pogorel'tsevs should be carefully compared with housefire motifs in Dostoevsky's works, including especially Dmitrii Karamazov's dream about the fire victims (*pogorel'tsy*), a dream which he calls "a prophecy" (*prorochestvo*) [Book 11, Part 4].
11 Note the juxtaposition of words in this passage of Chapter 3:
> [Trusotskii:] "...I'm in such a state of *spirit*... and I've been mentally broken since March..."
>
> "Ah, yes! Broken since March... Wait a minute. Do you *smoke*?"

12 See Kirpotin, pp.168-246.

LIBRARY OF DAVIDSON

Books on regular loan may b
must be presented at th